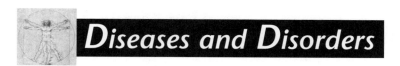

Diseases and Disorders

Headaches

by Barbara Sheen

LUCENT
BOOKS ®

THOMSON
—✦—
™
GALE

San Diego • Detroit • New York • San Francisco • Cleveland
New Haven, Conn. • Waterville, Maine • London • Munich

For more information, contact
Lucent Books
27500 Drake Rd.
Farmington Hills, MI 48331-3535
Or you can visit our Internet site at www.gale.com

LIBRARY OF CONGRESS CATALOGING-IN-PUBLICATION DATA

Sheen, Barbara.
    Headaches / by Barbara Sheen.
        v. cm. — (Diseases and disorders series)
Includes bibliographical references and index.
Contents: What is a Headache?—Diagnosis and treatment—Alternative and comple-
mentary treatments—Living with Headaches—What the future holds.
    ISBN 1-59018-346-0 (hardback : alk. paper)
    I. Title. II. Series.

Table of Contents

"The Most Difficult Puzzles Ever Devised"

CHARLES BEST, ONE of the pioneers in the search for a cure for diabetes, once explained what it is about medical research that intrigued him so. "It's not just the gratification of knowing one is helping people," he confided, "although that probably is a more heroic and selfless motivation. Those feelings may enter in, but truly, what I find best is the feeling of going toe to toe with nature, of trying to solve the most difficult puzzles ever devised. The answers are there somewhere, those keys that will solve the puzzle and make the patient well. But how will those keys be found?"

Since the dawn of civilization, nothing has so puzzled people—and often frightened them, as well—as the onset of illness in a body or mind that had seemed healthy before. A seizure, the inability of a heart to pump, the sudden deterioration of muscle tone in a small child—being unable to reverse such conditions or even to understand why they occur was unspeakably frustrating to healers. Even before there were names for such conditions, even before they were understood at all, each was a reminder of how complex the human body was, and how vulnerable.

While our grappling with understanding diseases has been frustrating at times, it has also provided some of humankind's most heroic accomplishments. Alexander Fleming's accidental discovery in 1928 of a mold that could be turned into penicillin has resulted in the saving of untold millions of lives. The isolation of the enzyme insulin has reversed what was once a death sentence for anyone with diabetes. There have been great strides in combating conditions for which there is not yet a cure, too. Medicines can help AIDS patients live longer, diagnostic tools such as mammography and ultrasounds can help doctors find tumors while they are treatable, and laser surgery techniques have made the most intricate, minute operations routine.

This "toe-to-toe" competition with diseases and disorders is even more remarkable when seen in a historical continuum. An astonishing amount of progress has been made in a very short time. Just two hundred years ago, the existence of germs as a cause of some diseases was unknown. In fact, it was less than 150 years ago that a British surgeon named Joseph Lister had difficulty persuading his fellow doctors that washing their hands before delivering a baby might increase the chances of a healthy delivery (especially if they had just attended to a diseased patient)!

Each book in Lucent's Diseases and Disorders series explores a disease or disorder and the knowledge that has been accumulated (or discarded) by doctors through the years. Each book also examines the tools used for pinpointing a diagnosis, as well as the various means that are used to treat or cure a disease. Finally, new ideas are presented—techniques or medicines that may be on the horizon.

Frustration and disappointment are still part of medicine, for not every disease or condition can be cured or prevented. But the limitations of knowledge are being pushed outward constantly; the "most difficult puzzles ever devised" are finding challengers every day.

Headaches—A Costly Complaint

UNA BEGAN GETTING headaches when she was thirteen. "At first," she explains, "they were few and far between but [over time] . . . they became worse and more frequent. I went to my doctor and was diagnosed with migraine [a type of headache]."[1]

During the next few years, Una's headaches worsened. By the time she reached her final year of high school, she had been hospitalized twice due to debilitating headaches and missed over six weeks of school in one year. In fact, because of her headaches, Una doubted whether she would be able to pass her final exams and graduate.

Like Una, over 45 million Americans suffer from habitual, recurring headaches. This is more than the number of Americans with either heart disease, asthma, or diabetes. Indeed, at any one time, an estimated 20 million Americans are experiencing a headache.

Although headaches are not usually life threatening, they do take a physical, emotional, and financial toll on people's lives. Headaches cause pain and powerlessness, interfere with families, school, and careers, and lower the quality of life for the sufferers and their families. For example, according to the National Headache Foundation, 53 percent of headache sufferers report having to retire to their beds because their headaches are so severe. This behavior has an emotional impact not only on the sufferer, but also on his or her family, causing them to feel frustrated, disappointed, and worried. The son of Clinton, a headache sufferer, recalls: "I remember trips having to be canceled and missing out on doing things. It was hard to make plans because we kids couldn't drive and our mother didn't drive on freeways. One time Dad was supposed to take a group of kids to a movie and he got a headache, so that was the end of that plan."[2]

This same behavior causes many people with headaches to miss work or school. American children miss an estimated 329,000 school days each year due to headaches. In fact, the National Headache Foundation estimates 10 million children between the ages of five and seventeen get recurrent headaches. Therefore, it is not surprising that 20 percent of all people with headaches got their first headache before age ten or that 75 percent of all American children have had at least one serious headache by age fifteen.

The picture is even bleaker when it comes to missed workdays. Recurrent headaches are the chief cause of lost productivity in the United States. According to the National Headache Foundation, an estimated 157 million workdays per year are lost to headaches. This translates to more than $13 billion a year in lost wages and lost business revenues, and does not include the estimated five days per month that people work while experiencing a headache, which causes the quality of their work to suffer. Moreover, when medical costs are added to the picture, this sum jumps to $50 billion. Hence, it is not surprising that headaches are the number one reason that people visit their doctors each year or that approximately 2.5 percent of all emergency room visits are for headaches.

What is surprising is the millions of headache sufferers who do not seek medical help. Experts believe this is because many sufferers lack knowledge of their disease and wrongly believe that there is no treatment available to relieve their headache pain.

Moreover, many people with headaches avoid seeking help in order to escape the stigma associated with the disease. This is because society has not always viewed headaches as a serious medical condition. Instead, headaches have often been viewed as a nervous condition that people can control if they want to. Even today, some people believe that headaches are not a biological

Forty-five million Americans suffer from recurring headaches. The chronic pain of these headaches affects virtually every aspect of the sufferer's life.

disease. This misconception has kept many people from getting medical treatment.

Even when headache sufferers seek medical help, many do not receive sympathy or support from their families, friends, or coworkers. Many people do not understand the pain that people with recurrent, severe headaches endure. Instead, they confuse the pain of these severe headaches with the minor headaches that most people experience occasionally. Cindy, a headache sufferer explains, "People hear the word headache and immediately think 'Tylenol'. And I think oh terrific! A Band-Aid for a bullet wound!"[3]

In order to provide headache sufferers with the support they need, as well as lessen the financial toll headaches have on society, it is important that people learn more about headaches. By learning what triggers headaches, how they are treated, and what challenges living with them present, headache patients can make better choices about their treatment and learn ways to manage and control their condition. At the same time, by becoming better informed, friends and family members will be better able to understand what their loved one is going through and thus provide him or her with much-needed support. Indeed, once Una learned more about headaches, she became more confident and better able to cope. As a result, she graduated from high school and is optimistically looking to the future.

Chapter 1

What Is a Headache?

J UST AS THE name implies, a headache is a pain in all or part of the head that may also be felt in the face and neck. A headache can be a symptom of disease, in which case it is known as a secondary headache. Infectious diseases, such as the common cold, influenza, and pneumonia, often produce secondary headaches, as does an allergic reaction or a sinus infection. Secondary headaches are also a symptom of the eye disease glaucoma, high blood pressure, stroke, head injury, a brain tumor, and a teeth-grinding condition known as temporomandibular joint (TMJ) syndrome.

Ninety percent of all headaches, however, are unrelated to any other medical condition. These headaches are called primary headaches. Primary headaches may be episodic, which means they occur occasionally, or they may be chronic. Chronic headaches strike at least four times a month and usually affect a person for most or all of his or her life. Debbie, one woman who has had chronic headaches for more than twenty years, describes her experience: "I started getting headaches in my early twenties. A lot of times, I wake up in the middle of the night with a bad headache. I get them at work too. I try to ignore them and go on with whatever I have to do. But since I get headaches about three or four times a week, it's hard. That's more than three thousand headaches in the last twenty years."[4]

Headache Causes

Scientists do not know exactly what causes headaches, but there are a number of theories on the subject. The most widely accepted theory is that headaches are caused by biochemical and blood-flow changes in the brain. According to this theory, headaches occur when an individual's nervous system reacts abnormally to otherwise harmless substances that he or she may eat, see, smell, hear, or feel. These substances are known as headache triggers.

When exposed to these triggers, the nervous system responds by producing a spasm in the arteries at the base of the brain. This causes the affected arteries to narrow or constrict, making it difficult for oxygen-rich blood to flow through the arteries and reach the brain. Therefore, the brain's supply of oxygen and blood is reduced. When the arteries narrow, blood cells called platelets can no longer move easily through the bloodstream. As a result, the platelets jam together. When they do, they become sticky and their walls become damaged, causing chemicals stored within them to leak out into the bloodstream.

One of these chemicals is serotonin. Serotonin is a neurotransmitter or chemical messenger. Like all neurotransmitters, serotonin

This cross-section of an artery shows free blood flow. When exposed to headache triggers, the arteries narrow and restrict the flow of blood to the brain.

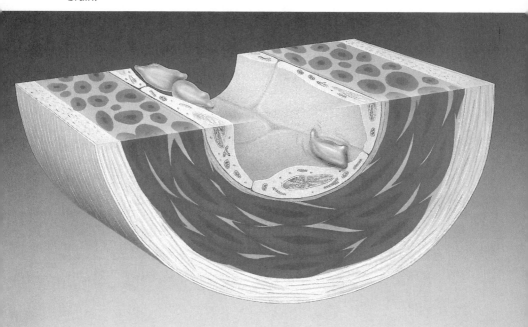

is involved in carrying messages to the brain. These messages involve mood, sleep, pain production, and the widening and narrowing of blood vessels.

High levels of serotonin in the bloodstream signal the brain to act in a prescribed manner. Conversely, low levels signal the brain to act in an opposing manner. For example, high levels of serotonin signal the brain to constrict blood vessels and limit the body's response to pain. Low levels of serotonin, on the other hand, cause the blood vessels to widen and make the body more sensitive to pain. Therefore, when platelets leak excess serotonin into the bloodstream, the blood vessels are forced to narrow further. This results in an even greater decrease in the amount of oxygen and blood that reaches the brain.

Faced with a lack of blood and oxygen, the nervous system once again overreacts and suppresses the production of serotonin. Lack of serotonin causes blood vessels to widen, and makes the body more sensitive to pain. At the same time, the immune system responds by sending chemicals to the brain that cause inflammation and swelling. These chemicals cause other arteries within the brain to swell. The combination of narrowing and widening blood vessels, the presence of inflammation, and fluctuating serotonin levels cause a squeezing or throbbing pain in the head—a headache.

Different Types of Headaches

There are over 150 different types of headaches. The most common are tension, migraine, and cluster headaches, all of which are primary headaches. Of these, tension headaches affect the most people. In fact, according to headache expert and doctor of internal medicine Joel Paulino, tension headaches are the cause of 90 percent of all chronic, primary headache pain in the United States. In addition, an estimated 95 percent of people in the United States experience episodic tension headaches at one time or another.

Tension Headaches

Tension headaches are the least severe form. However, some people get chronic tension headaches on a daily basis, and this

Types of Headaches

	Tension	Migraine	Cluster
Type of Pain	steady, dull	severe, throbbing	severe, sharp
Location of Pain	both sides of head and neck	usually on one side of head	around one eye
Who Is Affected	both males and females	mostly females	mostly males

pattern of headaches can persist for years. Characterized by mild to moderate pain, tension headaches produce a persistent ache that makes people feel like their heads are being squeezed tightly. These headaches usually affect both sides of the head, as well as the part of the head where the head and neck muscles meet. Paulino describes how tension headaches made Juan, one of his patients, feel. The headaches, he explains, "led to a buildup of pain and tightness in his forehead and the back of his head and neck. Sometimes the pain felt like a tight band around his head." Juan told Paulino: "It feels like my head is held in a vise."[5]

Migraine Headaches

Migraine headaches are the second most common form of primary headaches, affecting 23 million Americans. Migraine headaches are usually more painful and more debilitating than tension headaches.

Unlike tension headache pain, migraine headaches usually affect only one side of the head, but may occur on the opposite side during another attack. Migraine pain can range from moderate to unbearable and is most often described as a throbbing or hammering pain. According to Lucy a migraine sufferer, "A migraine is like a freight train, a rugby game, and a mining operation, all going on and through your head at once."[6]

In addition to causing pain in the head, migraine headaches usually cause nausea and vomiting. This frequently makes it difficult for people with migraines to function. Dina describes what a migraine is like: "When I get a migraine, I can't function. I have to lay down with no lights and no noise. Before it is over, I start throwing up. Throwing up makes it worse, makes my head hurt more. It's horrible."[7]

Cluster Headaches

The third type of primary headaches is cluster headaches. Less common than tension or migraine headaches, cluster headaches affect about 2 million Americans. Said by both patients and doctors to be among the most painful of all headaches, cluster headaches typically appear in cycles or clusters. They usually strike five or six times a day for several consecutive days, weeks, or even months, then cease, only to return in the future. Approximately 10 to 20 percent of cluster headache patients have a form of cluster headaches that lasts more than a year and disappears for less than two weeks before returning. According to neurologist Peter Goadsby, director of the Headache Group of London's Institute of Neurology, "Cluster headache is probably the worst pain that humans experience. I know that's quite a strong remark to make, but if you ask a cluster headache patient if they've had a worse experience, they'll universally say they haven't."[8]

Typically, cluster headaches begin and end suddenly. The pain, which is often described as sharp and stabbing, usually comes from behind one eye and affects only one side of the head, but may affect the opposite side during another attack. "They come on very rapidly," John, a cluster sufferer, explains:

> You suddenly realize that you have a pain behind your eye. . . . As soon as you get the first twinge you know that within five minutes you may lose control of yourself and be reduced to whimpering. . . . Violent pain doesn't generally last; if you bang your head against something it hurts for a moment then it subsides. It just doesn't subside with a cluster headache, it goes on . . . and then all of a sudden it stops.[9]

Headache Triggers

No matter what type of headache a person gets, exposure to specific headache triggers stimulates an individual's nervous system to react abnormally. Although headache triggers do not cause headaches, they do induce the chain of events that produce a headache in certain people. Scientists say that some people are more sensitive to headache triggers than others and thus are more susceptible to headaches. But they do not know why this is so. Scientists do know that most headache triggers are dietary, environmental, hormonal, or connected to a person's lifestyle.

Dietary Triggers

Dietary triggers are common headache triggers. In fact, it is estimated that 30 percent of all headache triggers are dietary. Almost any food or beverage can be a headache trigger. However, certain dietary triggers are more common than others. Among these are nitrates, which are chemicals found in processed meats such as hot dogs, sausage, salami, and bologna. At high doses, nitrates are known to dilate the blood vessels. In fact, the medicine nitroglycerin, which is used to treat heart patients with constricted blood vessels, is a nitrate. Although the amount of nitrates found in processed meat has no effect on the blood vessels of most people, scientists think that even low doses of nitrates may affect the blood vessels of susceptible people.

Other common dietary triggers include chemicals known as amines; the food additive MSG, or monosodium glutamate; and the food preservative sulfite. Amines are commonly found in chocolate, cheese, yogurt, red wine, raisins, tuna, salmon, tomatoes, citrus fruit, and legumes such as beans, nuts, peas, and soy products. MSG is often used in oriental cooking, while sulfites are found in dried fruit and alcoholic beverages. Scientists do not know why these substances trigger headaches. They theorize that certain people are unable to break down these substances when they ingest them, which affects their blood vessels.

Environmental Triggers

Environmental triggers also affect many headache sufferers. These include air pollutants, weather changes, certain odors,

Chemicals called nitrates commonly found in processed meats like these sausages are a common headache trigger.

bright lights, and loud noises. Air pollutants like smoke and gasoline fumes, for example, raise carbon monoxide levels in the air while lowering oxygen levels. Although breathing in polluted air is not healthy for anyone, for people susceptible to headaches, even minor changes in the amount of oxygen inhaled, and thus the amount that enters the bloodstream, can trigger a headache. Debbie, a sufferer whose headaches are triggered by air pollution, describes her experience: "Pollutants in the air always give me a headache. The other day I went to the airport to pick up my daughter. That night I woke up at 2:00 A.M. with a terrible headache from the pollutants in the air in El Paso [the city where the airport is located]. My head hurt all day."[10]

Other environmental triggers, like weather changes, include not only changes in temperature, but also changes in air pressure and humidity. According to doctor of internal medicine and headache expert Dennis Fox, 43 percent of headache patients report that weather changes trigger their headaches. High winds in particular appear to be a widespread trigger. Scientists theorize that this may be due to electrical changes in the air, which somehow may affect serotonin production in susceptible people.

Bright lights and glare from sunlight, fluorescent lights, or a television or computer screen also are common environmental triggers. Bright lights stimulate the brain, as well as cause people to tense muscles around their eyes and forehead in order to squint or block out light. Both these factors may prompt the arteries in the head to spasm and thus induce a headache. Loud noises and powerful odors, too, stimulate the brain and cause people to tense muscles in the face and head. Strong perfumes seem to trigger headaches in many people. Headache expert and neurologist Christina Peterson explains: "Highly complex perfumes with many aromatic components tend to pose the biggest problems, along with heavy, spicy perfumes. I avoid wearing most perfumes to the office, as I would hate to trigger someone's migraine."[11]

Hormonal Triggers

Another common headache trigger is hormonal changes in a person's body. Hormonal changes are often associated with puberty, a woman's menstrual cycle, and pregnancy. Experts say that fluctuations in the level of hormones, chemicals produced by the body, may also affect serotonin production. Therefore, it is not surprising that many young women start getting headaches during puberty, or that many pregnant women suffer from headaches, since these are both times when a female's hormones rise and fall frequently. Indeed, scientists have proven that in the days before a woman's menstrual period begins, levels of the female hormone estrogen fall. Interestingly, low levels of estrogen have been linked to a decrease in serotonin production. This may be the reason many women report getting headaches in the days before the start of their menstrual period. Cindy, who suffers from premenstrual headaches, explains: "I always know when a headache is coming on. It always starts about thirty-six hours before my period arrives. I start taking Tylenol before it [the headache] starts, because I know it will."[12]

Common Headache Triggers

- **Caffeine**
- **Alcohol**
- **Chocolate**
- **Stress**
- **Noise**
- **Pollution**
- **Odors**
- **Weather changes**
- **Change in hormone levels**

Lifestyle Triggers

Certain lifestyle factors also are known to trigger headaches. These include lack of food, intense exercise, stress, and irregular sleep patterns. Intense exercise and skipping meals can cause blood sugar levels to drop. Low blood sugar causes the body to release the hormones adrenaline and cortisol that, like the hormone estrogen, are linked to a decrease in serotonin production. In addition, the presence of these hormones increases a person's sensitivity to pain. Debbie, whose headaches are not only triggered by air pollution but also by lack of food, explains: "If I don't eat right, or if I go too long without eating, I get a real bad headache. When I start getting a headache, one of the first things I ask myself is when I last ate."[13]

Stress, too, causes the body to release adrenaline and cortisol into the bloodstream. Therefore, it is not surprising that stress is a widespread headache trigger. In fact, stress is the most common of all headache triggers, responsible for approximately 63 percent of all headaches.

Irregular sleep patterns also trigger headaches in some people. A study at Case Western Reserve University in Cleveland, Ohio, of children with migraines, for example, reported in the April 2003 issue of *Headache: The Journal of Head and Face Pain*, that 42 percent of the subjects did not get enough sleep. Scientists do not know why irregular sleep patterns trigger headaches but theorize that they affect the working of the brain and cause fluctuations in serotonin levels.

Multiple Triggers

Most headache patients are sensitive to multiple triggers. When a person is exposed to a number of triggers simultaneously, his or her chance of developing a headache becomes greater, as does the severity of the headache. The reason for this is that the more triggers, the more powerful the effect. Complicating matters, trigger combinations can vary at different times. For instance, a person may be sensitive to wine, loud noise, stress, and air pollution. If the person is exposed to loud noise alone, a headache may not develop. But if the person drinks wine in a noisy, smoky bar, the chance of a headache developing increases significantly. At another time, the same person might react to a different combination, and for those people who are sensitive to a wide number of triggers, the combinations can be extensive.

People at Risk

No matter what triggers a headache, it is clear that almost everyone gets one occasionally. Headaches strike people of all ages, races, and genders. However, certain people are at risk of developing chronic headaches. One such group of people is women. Migraine headaches, in particular, seem to strike women more frequently than they do men. Of the 23 million migraine patients in the United States, 18 million are women. Moreover, most of these women are between twenty and fifty years old. This is typically the time in a woman's life when she experiences fluctuating hormone levels tied to her menstrual cycle, which experts theorize play a great role in putting women at risk. Conversely, men are at a six-times greater risk than women of developing cluster headaches. Scientists cannot explain why.

Genetics

Both males and females who have family members with chronic headaches are also at risk. All types of headaches, and migraines in particular, appear to run in families. According to Paulino, between 70 and 80 percent of all migraine patients have family members with migraines. Scientists have not yet found a specific gene that causes or predisposes people to headaches. However, based on statistics of multiple family members with headaches, scientists theorize that some people inherit a sensitivity to headache triggers, which makes them more susceptible to headaches. Cindy describes how headaches affect her husband's family: "My husband's brother has migraines, so does his sister, her daughter, and now her son. Recently, our son said he had a migraine too."[14]

Physical Effects of Headaches

No matter who gets them, headaches have a physical impact. Headaches affect the brain and central nervous system. Since the central nervous system is the command center of the body, when there are problems here a ripple effect is produced throughout the body. For example, when a headache is occurring, nerve cells (neurons) in the brain often receive faulty messages and, in turn, release neurotransmitters that carry these faulty messages to the rest of the body. Therefore, the physical impact of headaches is felt not only in the head, face, and neck, but throughout the whole body.

For this reason, headaches can cause nausea; vomiting; dizziness; fatigue; sensitivity to light, sound, and smell; numbness; nasal congestion; facial swelling; tearing; and swelling and drooping of the eyelids. Although these problems generally subside when the headache ends, frequent vomiting can cause permanent damage. Since vomit is extremely acidic, frequent vomiting can damage the lining of the throat, mouth, and esophagus, and has been linked to cancer in these areas.

Emotional Effects of Headaches

Besides having a physical effect, headaches also have an emotional effect. Because headaches can be so painful and disruptive, many

Effects of Headaches

Besides pain, people with headaches may experience:

- **Nausea**
- **Dizziness**
- **Fatigue**
- **Sensitivity to light, sound, and smell**
- **Nasal congestion**
- **Anxiety**
- **Depression**

people with chronic headaches report feeling sad and resentful about the toll headaches take on their lives. They also report feeling chronic anxiety about when and where a headache will strike. Indeed, according to Fox, 60 percent of chronic headache patients suffer from chronic anxiety. Laura, a headache sufferer, explains: "One of the worst parts is the fear of when it [a headache] will rear its ugly head. You never know when you're going to lose twenty-four hours or forty-eight hours. Where am I going to be when it hits? Will I be driving my car? At my sister's wedding? It's the not knowing that's almost worse than the pain."[15]

Feelings of anxiety, resentfulness, and sadness cause many headache patients to become depressed. When people are depressed, they feel tired, have trouble sleeping and concentrating, and lack an interest in everyday life. Indeed, depression is more common among headache patients than among the general population. According to Fox, 30 percent of chronic headache patients suffer from depression. The statistics are even higher among migraine patients. According to a joint British and American study led by neurologist Dr. Richard Lipton of the Albert Einstein Institute in Bronx, New York, in 2000,

47 percent of migraine sufferers are affected by depression. In fact, researchers think that there is a direct link between headaches and depression. They do not know whether this link is strictly emotional or if decreased serotonin levels, which are involved in causing both headaches and depression, play a role.

Of course, not every headache patient suffers from depression. However, because severe or chronic headaches take a physical and emotional toll on people's lives, it is important that people suffering from them seek medical help.

Chapter 2

Diagnosis and Treatment

DIAGNOSING THE TYPE of headaches a person experiences can be difficult. First, the doctor must determine whether the headaches are primary or secondary. Making this determination is important, since secondary headaches can be a symptom of any number of diseases that, if left untreated, often have grave consequences. A stroke, blood clot, brain tumor, or head injury, for example, can be life threatening.

Moreover, since there are no medical tests to diagnose primary headaches, differentiating between primary and secondary headaches can be problematic. However, doctors can diagnose most secondary headaches via medical imaging tests, such as magnetic resonance imaging, or MRI, and computerized axial tomography, or CAT scan. Therefore, in order to eliminate the possibility of secondary headaches, medical imaging tests are administered. Once the specific type of headache is determined, treatment can begin.

Testing

Both an MRI and a CAT scan can reveal brain tumors, stroke, blood clots, sinus problems, and head injury that can cause secondary headaches. Unlike traditional X rays that take pictures of bone, a CAT scan and an MRI take pictures of soft tissue. These tests are very similar and both are painless. However, an MRI is more sensitive and can detect small brain tumors and blood clots that a CAT scan may miss. During these tests, the patient lies on a special moving table that passes through an imaging machine

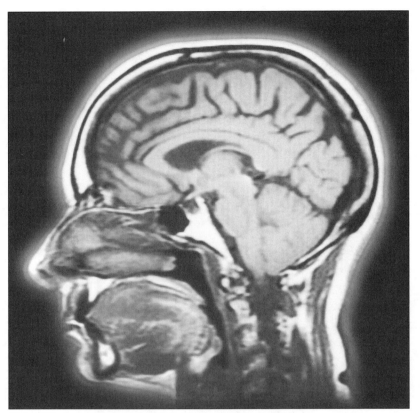

This MRI shows the soft tissue inside a person's skull. MRIs are used to diagnose brain tumors, blood clots, and other serious problems that can cause secondary headaches.

that takes detailed, three-dimensional pictures of—in the case of headaches—the patient's brain. The pictures are viewed on a computer monitor, which improves their sharpness and clarity. Abnormal features, such as a dark mass that indicates a brain tumor, will appear if the patient has secondary headaches. If this is the case, the doctor then treats the underlying condition causing the headaches. If, however, there are no abnormalities, secondary headaches are ruled out and primary headaches are indicated.

Once primary headaches are diagnosed, before they can be treated, the doctor must ascertain which type of primary headache a patient has. This is because treatment for different types of primary headaches varies. Examining specific symptoms helps the doctor to make this diagnosis.

Symptoms of Tension Headaches

When patients report that their headaches begin gradually, strike when they are awake, and are unaccompanied by nausea or vomiting, tension headaches are indicated. People with tension headaches also report that the pain is dull rather than throbbing. The pain may be mild to moderate and is commonly felt on both sides of the forehead, the neck, and the back of the head.

Symptoms of Cluster Headaches

Like tension headaches, cluster headaches rarely are accompanied by nausea or vomiting. But unlike tension headaches, cluster headaches usually strike while a person is asleep, and the piercing pain wakes the victim up. Accompanying symptoms include swelling, redness, and tearing of the eye on the affected side of the head as well as facial swelling. In addition, the eyelid of the affected eye tends to droop, and the nostril on the affected side of the head becomes congested. Cluster headaches also cause feelings of extreme restlessness and agitation. In fact, it is not uncommon for people to pace rapidly during a cluster headache attack. When patients report these symptoms, the diagnosis is cluster headaches.

Jeff, a headache sufferer, describes his symptoms during one attack: "I was awakened from my sleep. . . . My right eye felt like I took a couple of punches, and my right nostril was starting to leak. I got out of bed, and went downstairs, all the while, this pressure in the right side of my brain kept building and building. My right eyelid was beginning to swell shut. I was squinting and it was tearing. I was pacing from room to room . . . and I suffered."[16]

Symptoms of Migraine Headaches

Unlike tension and cluster headaches, migraine headaches occur in three stages. The presence of specific symptoms characteristic of each stage helps doctors in the diagnosis. For example, the first stage, known as the prodrome or warning stage, occurs before the actual headache begins. During this stage, patients report such symptoms as chills, abdominal pain, yawning, loss of appetite, inability to concentrate, frequent urination, thirst, and mood changes. This stage almost always occurs while the patient is awake. Jane, a migraine sufferer, describes her symptoms during the prodrome stage: "I have several hints that a migraine is coming. Excessive urination and excessive yawning are two of them. I also seem to have either a lot more or a lot less energy than usual. Sometimes I am in a black mood beforehand."[17]

During the prodrome stage, approximately 20 percent of migraine patients experience auras. An aura is a visual disturbance

A woman experiences the severe pain of a migraine headache. Migraines occur in three stages: the warning stage, the headache stage, and the postdrome stage.

that scientists do not know the cause of. It appears in the form of blind spots, flashing lights, shooting stars, or zigzag lines, which occur in one eye. An aura can last up to an hour, but typically auras last no more than thirty minutes. When auras end, the second stage, which is the actual headache, begins. "Usually before the headache starts off," Drew, a migraine sufferer explains, "I have blurriness in my right eye. It's really weird, really blurry like in a weird dream. Then I can't see out of my eye at all. Then a half-hour later the headache starts."[18]

As the name implies, during the headache stage, the actual head pain occurs. Also during this stage, most migraine patients report sensitivity to light, sound, and smells as well as experiencing nausea and vomiting. Jill, a migraine sufferer, explains: "When you have a headache, even paper has a smell. And smells can be so intense as to be devastating."[19]

The headache stage can last from four to seventy-two hours. When the headache stage ends, it is followed by the postdrome stage during which headache pain and associated symptoms disappear. Most people report feeling fatigued during this stage, and many sleep.

Different Treatment for Different Headaches

Once the doctor analyzes the patient's symptoms and makes a diagnosis, deciding what type of treatment will be best for each individual is not simple. The doctor must consider not only the type of headache, but also the severity and frequency of the headaches in order to prescribe an appropriate treatment. In some diseases, such as asthma and acne, doctors have a special scale that helps them analyze the severity of a person's illness and match the results to specific treatments. However, there is no such scale to analyze these factors for headaches. Therefore, doctors must determine what treatment is best for the patient based on symptoms and medical history.

Information that the doctor considers includes the length and timing of a patient's headaches. Long-lasting headaches, for example, require longer-acting medication; headaches tied to a woman's menstrual cycle may be helped with special hormonal treatments. The doctor also considers whether the headaches are accompanied by nausea and vomiting, which require medication to ease these side effects. Then, before prescribing a drug, the doctor must factor in whether the patient is allergic to any medications, suffers from high blood pressure or heart disease (conditions that some headache medication can worsen), and takes medication for illnesses, such as asthma for instance, with which some headache medications can interfere.

Since these factors can differ greatly from patient to patient, headache treatment also varies. However, no matter what sort of treatment is prescribed, the goal remains the same—to lessen the frequency and severity of headaches. Health writer Diane Stafford explains: "Today doctors have a huge arsenal of headache drugs that can prevent a migraine [and other headaches] from getting worse, stop head pain in its tracks, [and] make recurrences less likely."[20]

Headache Medication

There are two types of medicines to treat headaches: abortive medicines and preventive medicines. Abortive medicines treat headache symptoms. They are taken once a headache strikes to lessen pain and treat associated symptoms. Preventive medicine is taken on a daily basis in an effort to lessen or stop headaches from occurring.

Abortive Medicines

Depending on the severity and frequency of a person's headaches, abortive medicines can range from mild, over-the-counter medications, which can be purchased without a doctor's prescription, to powerful, prescription-strength painkillers. Over-the-counter medications are taken orally. Known as analgesics, these medications relieve pain by reducing inflammation, which, in the case of headaches, translates into a reduction in the swelling of blood vessels. Common over-the-counter analgesics include aspirin, naproxen, acetaminophen, and ibuprofen. Some analgesics also contain caffeine, which causes swollen blood vessels to narrow. In general, because they are not very powerful, over-the-counter medicines work best on mild, tension headaches. Therefore, doctors rarely prescribe them for patients who suffer from more severe headaches. Debbie talks about how over-the-counter analgesics affect her: "Sometimes if I take Excedrin [a brand-name over-the-counter analgesic consisting of a combination of acetaminophen, aspirin, and caffeine] at the beginning of a mild headache, it will be better. But when the headache is bad, I can take twenty aspirins and it wouldn't do any good."[21]

For severe headaches, stronger medication is often needed. Such medication includes triptans, a family of drugs that attach to serotonin receptors in the brain. There they stimulate serotonin receptors to attract serotonin, which helps limit the body's response to pain and reduces nausea and vomiting. At the same time, chemicals in triptans reduce inflammation around blood vessels. There are a number of different varieties of triptan-based medications, including sumatriptan, naratriptan, zolmitriptan, and rizatriptan. These drugs may be taken orally, in the form of

Many headache sufferers use over-the-counter analgesics like aspirin or ibuprofen to relieve pain.

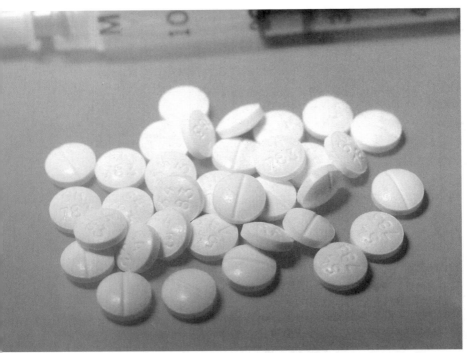

For patients who do not respond to other medications, doctors often prescribe opiates like these codeine tablets to alleviate pain.

a nasal spray, or via injection, and are usually quite effective at relieving headache pain and the related nausea. Many people report having only mild or no pain two hours after taking triptan. Dana, a headache sufferer, describes how Imitrex, a brand name for sumatriptan, helps her: "I love that Imitrex . . . Imitrex allows me to function. The pain often goes away in fifteen minutes with no downtime."[22]

However, not every patient responds to triptans. Headache experts estimate that triptans are effective in about 70 percent of all cases. And even when patients do respond to triptans, in cases where an individual's headache pain is extremely severe, such as in cluster headaches, triptans do not always provide enough relief to ease a patient's pain. Moreover, although triptans are fast acting, they are not long acting. They generally provide relief for anywhere from four to twelve hours. But many migraine and cluster patients have headaches that last well beyond this time frame. Therefore, the effects of triptans often wear off before these patients' headaches end.

For these people, opiates, extremely powerful narcotic painkillers, are often prescribed. Opiates include codeine, morphine, and oxycodone, to name just a few. These drugs increase the brain's production of serotonin, which lessens feelings of pain, as well as increasing the production of another neurotransmitter, dopamine, which makes the body feel relaxed and calm. In fact, opiates have a strong sedating effect on the body, which many headache patients welcome when pain is severe.

Preventive Medicines

Unlike abortive medicines, preventive medicines are not painkillers. Consequently, they do not relieve the symptoms of a headache in progress. Instead, preventive medicines work to balance the long-term biochemical workings of the body. This includes regulating blood vessels, balancing female hormone levels, and increasing serotonin production. As a result, the frequency of headaches is reduced and when headaches do strike, they are often less severe. This makes it easier for abortive drugs to work.

Since preventive medicines are a long-term treatment, they are rarely administered to people with episodic headaches. Instead, they are most often prescribed for people who have at least two or three severe headaches each month, as well as for people who do not respond to abortive medicine. But even for these patients, preventive drugs will not work immediately. They must be taken one or more times a day, every day, and must build up in the nervous system for about three weeks before they start to work. Once they take effect and individuals experience less frequent headaches, some preventive medication users may be able to taper off and eventually stop taking preventive medications; other patients may need to take them indefinitely. In either case, most patients remain on these drugs for at least a year.

There are a number of different types of preventive headache medications. Most are taken orally or via injection. The most common are beta blockers, calcium channel blockers, anticonvulsants, antidepressants, and female hormones.

The most popular are beta blockers, which work by attaching to cells known as beta receptors located on the tips of neurons—or nerve cells. By attaching to these cells, beta blockers block messages from the brain that signal the narrowing of blood vessels. This prevents the repeated dilation and constriction of blood vessels that leads to headache pain.

Calcium channel blockers have a similar effect on blood vessels. However, calcium channel blockers do not attach to the tips of the neurons. Instead they attach to the walls of blood vessels, where they block calcium from passing through. For reasons that scientists do not completely understand, stopping the flow of calcium keeps blood vessels dilated and prevents headaches in some patients.

Anticonvulsants—which are also used to treat epilepsy, a disorder that causes seizures—also affect blood vessels. But anticonvulsants work by inhibiting electrical impulses that cause spasms in the arteries of the brain. By stopping these spasms, anticonvulsants hinder the chain of events that causes a headache. Anticonvulsants seem to be most effective for cluster headaches, although scientists do not know why this is so. Both beta blockers and calcium channel blockers are less effective for cluster headaches but work well on migraines; once again, scientists cannot explain why.

Antidepressants, too, are effective for migraines. They regulate the body's use and production of serotonin and other neurotransmitters such as dopamine, which are involved in mood and emotion, as well as regulating pain and blood vessels. Although antidepressants treat depression, because of their effect on serotonin regulation, they are prescribed both for headache patients who suffer from depression as well as those who do not. Peterson describes the effect of amitriptyline, an antidepressant, on one of her patients: "Heather . . . was plagued by severe migraines about once a week, lasting for a day or two. . . . Since starting on a nightly preventive dose of twenty-five milligrams of amitriptyline, Heather has had only one or two mild headaches a month."[23]

Among the medications used to prevent headaches are antidepressants like Paxil. Such medicines help reduce the frequency and severity of headache pain.

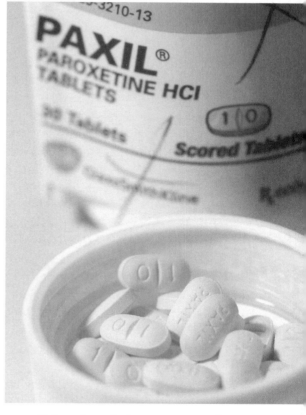

Unlike other preventive medicine, female hormones, such as estrogen, are prescribed only for female headache patients. Such medication does not prevent headaches in men due to the difference in men's body chemistry. But for women whose headaches appear to be tied to their menstrual cycle, by replacing depleted estrogen, hormone therapy balances hormonal levels and thus prevents headaches. Nita explains: "I had horrible incapacitating headaches. Nothing helped, and I tried everything. Once I started taking hormones, the headaches stopped. Since I've been on hormones, I haven't had a single headache."[24]

Risks and Side Effects of Headache Medications

Despite their benefits, like all medicines, medicines for headaches can present health risks and cause side effects. Some, such as beta blockers and calcium channel blockers, can cause a number of temporary problems like dizziness, fatigue, and light-headedness. Moreover, because these medications keep all blood vessels dilated, using these drugs can worsen conditions such as asthma, where constricted blood vessels in the lungs help filter out pollutants and other items that trigger asthma attacks; dilated blood vessels allow these substances easy access to the lungs and thus may encourage or worsen asthma attacks.

Over-the-counter analgesics, too, can cause temporary problems, like an upset stomach. Acid and chemicals in analgesics can also cause long-term health problems, such as gastrointestinal bleeding, stomach ulcers, and liver damage, especially when these drugs are taken in high doses. Triptans can be dangerous because they constrict blood vessels not only in the brain, but throughout the body. They can lead to heart attack or stroke, which occur when blood cannot pass through the constricted blood vessels leading to the heart or the brain. Even hormone therapy has its risks: It has been linked to the development of heart disease and breast cancer.

Opiates present other health risks. Besides causing constipation, loss of appetite, mood changes, and skin rashes, these drugs can be extremely addictive. Patients can quickly develop a physical and psychological dependence upon opiates and face painful withdrawal symptoms if they try to stop using them. Moreover, there is no exact minimum dosage that will guarantee addiction will not occur. Some patients may be able to use opiates occasionally without any problems, while others may become addicted after only two or three doses. Therefore, people who take opiates must be careful to limit the frequency and amount of their dosage. For this reason, many doctors frown on prescribing opiates for headache patients and generally administer them only as a last resort. Medical doctor and addiction expert Elizabeth Connell Henderson explains: "When the brain is exposed to opiates, physical tolerance and dependence develop, even at very low doses. It has been shown, for example, that hospital patients who are given even small doses of opiate medication for acute pain have a mini withdrawal syndrome even after the first dose."[25]

Rebound Headaches

Dependence on opiates can also lead to another problem, the development of rebound headaches. Overuse of analgesics and triptans, too, can have a similar effect. Rebound headaches are headaches that are caused by headache medication. Taking triptans, analgesics, or opiates three times a day for a period of five days in a row can cause the brain to develop a tolerance to these drugs' painkilling effect. Therefore, these medications become less and less effective. In order to get relief, patients must take more frequent and larger doses.

Also, scientists think that, like opiates, repeated doses of triptans and analgesics lower serotonin levels in the brain. Reduced serotonin causes blood vessels to constrict, which leads to the onset of new headaches. Again, to combat these rebound headaches, patients often take more painkilling medication, which only worsens matters and causes the rebound cycle to begin again. Suzanne Simmons, executive director of the National Headache Foundation, explains: "As the sufferer continues to

Headache medications often have side effects. Even triptan nasal sprays like this can cause stomachaches, heart attacks, or strokes.

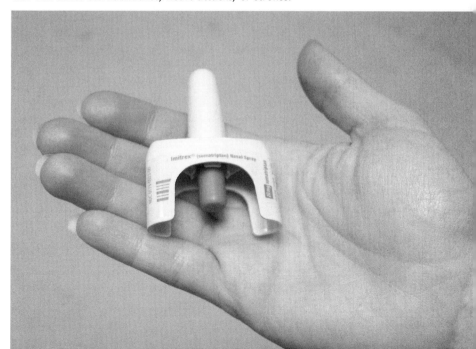

self medicate in search of headache relief, a vicious cycle develops and rebound headaches are often the painful result."[26]

Indeed, rebound headaches can be a big problem. According to Paulino, rebound headaches are the most common cause of chronic daily headaches in the United States. The only way to stop them is by discontinuing the use of the medication that causes them. However, since serotonin levels do not rise as soon as patients discontinue pain medication, headache pain does not cease. As a result, during this process, patients often endure severe headache pain for anywhere from a few days to two months. One headache sufferer talks about her experience:

> Everybody's taking something for headaches, and I was definitely gulping a lot of pills . . . when my fiancé took me to the emergency room, I was lying down in the car and my head was splitting—I really, truly thought I was dying. The doctor . . . told me I'd had a rebound or drug-induced headache. He said that both over-the-counter and prescription meds can cause rebounding if they are taken too often. . . . My doctor told me that . . . rebounding can be very painful and troublesome. He took me off these drugs, and it was two months before I finally quit having frequent headaches. Then, he helped me come up with a treatment plan that was much healthier and targeted my migraines better.[27]

Indeed, headache medication must be used cautiously. When patients work with their doctor and take headache medication only as it is prescribed, it can be effective in reducing the frequency and severity of their headaches and thus improve the quality of their lives.

Chapter 3

Alternative Treatments

S INCE HEADACHE MEDICATIONS can cause a number of health risks and side effects, and frequent use of some medications can cause painful rebound headaches, many headache patients turn to alternative treatments in hopes of reducing their usage of traditional headache medicines. Debbie, who turned to alternative treatment, explains: "The doctor gave me a lot of medicine that doped me up and made me feel like I was in a fog. The effect was as bad as the headaches. I threw that stuff out and I switched to an alternative supplement. It gave me more energy, and kept me calmer. After I'd been on it a while I mellowed out, and seemed to get fewer headaches."[28]

What Is Alternative Treatment?

An alternative treatment is a type of treatment that is not commonly accepted by traditional medical professionals in the United States. Due to limited studies that lack conclusive proof of their safety and effectiveness, most alternative treatments are not approved for use by the Federal Drug Administration (FDA). This is important, because when the FDA approves a treatment, the agency verifies that the advantages of the treatment exceed any possible health risks. And once a treatment is approved, the FDA regulates and sets standards for its use. Alternative treatments, on the other hand, generally are not regulated, and there are no set standards for their use.

In spite of these concerns, a large number of headache patients have found alternative treatments to be safe and effective in treating their headaches. In fact, a 2002 survey involving seventy-three headache patients at the Center for Oral, Facial and Head Pain at New York Presbyterian Hospital in New York City found that 85 percent of the patients surveyed used alternative treatments. Of the patients who reported using alternative treatments, 88 percent said these treatments were beneficial in relieving their headache pain.

Many medical professionals agree, especially when conventional drug treatment is combined with alternative treatments in a method known as complementary treatment. This combination, experts say, can reduce headache pain and lower stress, a key

Feverfew leaves contain natural chemicals that can prevent or reduce headache pain.

headache trigger. As a result, patients need less medication. Peterson explains: "I certainly do not discount alternative treatments altogether. In fact, while more study needs to be done into a number of them, I am the first to say that a combination of medication, lifestyle changes, and alternative remedies can yield better results for the management of migraine than medication alone."[29]

Alternative treatments for headaches fall into three categories: behavioral, hands-on, and herbal. Of these, herbal treatments have the longest history.

Herbal Treatment

Herbal treatments use the roots, stems, bark, or leaves of plants that are believed to have medicinal value to treat a wide range of illnesses, including headaches. Such treatments have been used for thousands of years. Indeed, feverfew, which is the most popular herbal treatment for headaches today, was used by the ancient Greeks to treat headaches.

Herbal experts say that feverfew contains natural chemicals that reduce inflammation, platelet clumping, and excess serotonin production, as well as preventing the arteries from going into spasms. Since all of these events are involved in the onset of a headache, if feverfew is taken daily for a few months, it may have the potential to prevent or lessen the frequency of headaches. And when feverfew is used as an abortive treatment, it may lessen the severity of headache pain. In fact, the U.S. Headache Consortium, a group of participants representing, among others, the American Academy of Neurology, the American Headache Society, the National Headache Foundation, and the American Academy of Family Physicians, analyzed data from three clinical studies on the effectiveness of feverfew in treating migraines. Based on the data, the consortium reported that feverfew may very well be an effective form of complementary preventive treatment for migraines and suggested that more research into the herb be undertaken.

Ginger is another popular herb used to treat headaches. Used since A.D. 500 in China and India, ginger is believed to reduce inflammation and platelet clotting as well as generally strengthening the body. In addition, a number of Chinese studies have shown it to inhibit nausea and vomiting. In fact, ginger is used in half of all Chinese herbal medicines as a way to settle the stomach and reduce inflammation. It is also commonly prescribed in India as well as in the West by practitioners of Ayurveda (traditional Indian medicine) for the treatment of headaches. Moreover, because of its antinausea properties, it is especially popular for treating migraines.

Although there are few studies on the effect of ginger on headaches, the Steven Foster Group, devoted to the study of herbs, reports on two studies at Southern Denmark University in Odense on ginger. These studies found that ginger indeed has anticoagulant properties, which means it can reduce platelet clumping and therefore may also provide relief from migraine pain and nausea. In fact, according to the group's website, researchers concluded that "Ginger may exert migraine-headache-relieving and preventive activity without side effects."[30]

Feverfew and ginger are not the only herbs used to treat headaches. Other herbs such as valerian root and Saint-John's-wort are commonly taken to ease anxiety, stress, and depression. Others, like ginkgo biloba, are used to increase blood flow.

Often a number of herbs are combined. Such is the case of lam kam sang heklin, a Chinese herbal supplement made from a variety of herbs. Produced under strict scientific conditions, lam kam sang heklin has been approved for sale in the United States by the FDA. According to the manufacturer, this product improves blood flow to the brain and inhibits the dilation and constriction of blood vessels that causes headache pain. In fact, the manufacturer claims that the product is 90 percent effective in reducing the frequency and severity of headaches after fifteen to sixty days of use.

Dr. Lam Kam Sang, director of the Lam Kam Sang Medical Research Institute in Hong Kong and developer of the product, describes the effect of the herbal combination on one of his patients:

> The pain often attacked at the temple and eye-socket at one side. It hurt so violently that she shed tears and nasal secretion incessantly. She had to take double dosage of anodyne [an opi-

ate pain reliever] and lie down in bed for about an hour for the pain to subside. The pain attacked two to three times a week. Both Chinese and Western medicine failed to make an improvement. . . . Heklin was prescribed for three times a day. In the first day of taking the medicine, the patient suffered an attack of the pain, but no anodyne was needed. After taking the Heklin for thirty-five days, the symptoms had completely disappeared. . . . No relapse has ever been found so far.[31]

Hands-on Treatments

Unlike herbal treatments, hands-on treatments involve the manipulation of the body to reduce pain and lower stress. Popular hands-on headache treatments include chiropractic care, massage therapy, reflexology, and acupuncture, with chiropractic care being among the most widely used.

Chiropractic

Chiropractic care is based on the theory that a misalignment of joints in the spine and neck interferes with the blood flow to the spinal cord and through the spinal cord to the brain. Since a reduction in blood flow to the brain occurs before a headache strikes, chiropractors say that by using gentle manipulation, such as rubbing, stroking, pressing, and stretching of muscles, to correct the misalignment of these bones, more oxygen and blood will reach the brain preventing or lessening headache pain. Although few studies exist on the effectiveness of chiropractic care for headaches, many patients find it effective. In particular, patients who suffer from tension headaches in which pain radiates to their necks, report chiropractic manipulation of their necks helps reduce the frequency of headaches and reduces headache pain. Peterson describes the case of one of her patients:

> Patty, forty-three, was reluctant to take preventive medications because of the side effects she's experienced with several. . . . [She] was referred to a chiropractor with special expertise in the treatment of headaches. Patty still has headaches, but now they occur just once or twice a month instead of once a week,

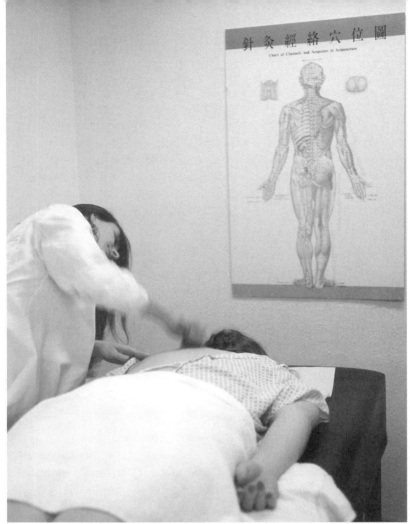

A chiropractor adjusts a patient's spine. Many headache sufferers find that chiropractic treatments reduce headache pain.

and they respond well to a compound analgesic [a mix of aspirin, acetaminophen, and caffeine, for example].[32]

Massage and Reflexology

Like chiropractic care, massage therapy involves the gentle rubbing, pressing, and stroking of the body. It is usually administered in a tranquil atmosphere that often includes soothing background music and the use of warm, scented massage oil to reduce friction. Massage has been proven to stimulate the brain to release endorphins, natural chemicals that produce feelings of well-being and diminish feelings of pain. Therefore, it is not surprising that many people report that massage therapy induces pleasurable feelings and relieves stress. Moreover, massage loosens tight muscles in the shoulders and neck, stimulates blood flow, relaxes the body, and relieves feelings of depression.

Massage can be administered to the whole body or to specific parts. A type of massage known as reflexology entails the massaging of the foot and ankle to relieve pain throughout the body. Reflexology is based on an ancient Chinese theory that blockages in an energy channel known as chi, which flows throughout the body, cause pain and illness. In order to clear these blockages, reflexologists massage specific zones in the foot, which they say correspond to all the organs in the body. For example, reflexologists maintain that massaging the toes clears blockages in the head and neck that cause headaches. Although

Massage therapy can be effective in reducing headaches because it stimulates natural chemicals in the body that diminish pain.

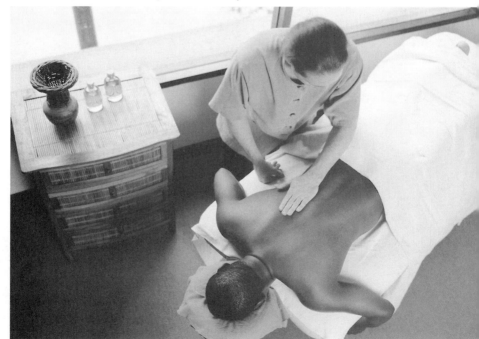

there is little scientific evidence that chi exists, reflexology appears to produce the same effect on the body as a full body massage. Therefore, after undergoing reflexology therapy, patients report feeling calmer and more relaxed as well as experiencing less headache pain. One patient declares: "Reflexology helped my migraines. They were very frequent, but now I can't remember the last time I had one."[33]

Acupuncture

Acupuncture is another ancient Chinese treatment that attempts to unblock chi. This is done through the insertion of very fine, sterile needles into specific points throughout the body. The needles are thought to activate the flow of energy through these points, which prevents or reduces pain. Although scientists are unsure why acupuncture relieves pain, many experts theorize that the insertion of acupuncture needles somehow stimulates the brain to release endorphins.

Acupuncture, an ancient Chinese treatment, uses very fine needles to activate the flow of energy to help relieve pain.

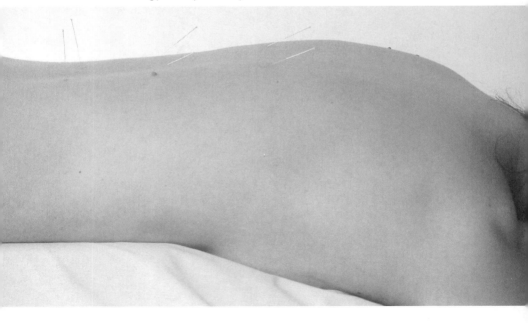

No matter why acupuncture relieves pain, a number of studies have shown that it is indeed an effective pain reliever. A 2002 study at the University of Turin, Italy, compared the effectiveness of treatment with acupuncture for migraines to treatment with flunarizine, a calcium channel blocker. In this study, 160 women with migraines were divided into two groups. One group received acupuncture treatments weekly for two months and then monthly for the next four months. The other group was given a daily dose of flunarizine for the first two months and then for twenty days per month for the next four months. In the first two months, the acupuncture group had significantly fewer headaches. After six months, no differences existed between the two groups. However, although both groups had fewer headaches after six months, only the acupuncture group reported a reduction in pain. In addition, the acupuncture group had fewer side effects.

However, like other alternative treatments, the practice of acupuncture is not regulated by the U.S. government. But since acupuncture has been shown to be so effective in treating headaches, the American Medical Association, the largest physician group in the United States, has approved acupuncture as an acceptable headache treatment. Therefore, it is not surprising that many traditional doctors recommend acupuncture to their headache patients as a complementary treatment, and many patients find it helps them. E., a migraine sufferer, talks about his experience: "I've suffered from migraine headaches for thirty years and have tried all sorts of medications that have been only partially effective. However, with acupuncture I have had effective (sometimes within minutes) relief from migraine pain. I don't fully understand how it works, but for relief of pain I highly recommend it."[34]

Behavioral Treatments

Unlike herbal and hands-on treatments that treat the body in order to control headaches, behavioral treatments train the mind to reduce feelings of pain and stress. Based on the theory that the mind influences the way the body functions, behavioral treatments include relaxation therapy, hypnosis, and biofeedback.

Relaxation

Just as the name implies, the goal of relaxation therapy is to help people relax and lessen their response to stress. This is achieved through a number of distinct methods that include relaxation tapes, meditation, and visualization, to name a few. Although each method is different, each employs specific mental techniques that relax the body.

Relaxation tapes, for instance, are special audiotapes that contain comforting background sounds, such as soft classical music or tinkling windchimes, to help listeners free their minds of worrisome thoughts. At the same time, voice instructions on the tape lead listeners through a program that teaches them how to relax their bodies. Through a series of exercises that include such activities as clenching and unclenching different muscles, patients learn how to relax their muscles, which lowers the body's response to stress and stress-induced headaches. Often used as a complementary form of treatment, according to many patients, relaxation tapes reduce their stress-induced headaches and thus lessen their need for abortive medicine. Debbie Jo, one patient, explains: "I'm a naturally tense person—your typical nervous Nellie. But when I learned how to relax myself, it helped immeasurably with my headaches. Now when I feel a migraine coming on, I turn to relaxation therapy first. It works for me at least half the time."[35]

Meditation and Visualization

Meditation and guided imagery are two other popular forms of relaxation therapy. Meditation involves clearing the mind in order to relax the body and relieve stress. To do this, meditators use a concentration technique in which they silently repeat a word or phrase until their mind is cleared and all stressful thoughts are gone. People who meditate report feeling deeply rested and relaxed after as little as twenty minutes of meditation. Indeed, research has shown that during meditation, the production of stress hormones such as cortisol and adrenaline decreases while serotonin levels increase. Moreover, when meditation is practiced often, these changes stabilize so that meditators' bodies react less strongly to stress during their daily life. The result is a lessening in headache frequency and severity.

Similarly, visualization uses the mind and the senses to relax the body. When practicing visualization, people construct a picture in their minds of a peaceful and safe place, such as a favorite vacation spot. They imagine the sights, sounds, and smells of the place. Then they picture themselves in that place, relaxed and pain free. By guiding their minds to this soothing and pain-free place, headache sufferers lower their response to stress and reduce their pain level. "Creative visualization can have a powerful effect on your behavior," explains Paulino. "When you think of yourself as a person without illness, you'll behave like a person free of illness. For example, if you have chronic headaches and see yourself without headaches, you'll likely be motivated to relax, even during stressful times."[36]

Hypnosis

Like meditation and visualization, hypnosis uses the mind to control the body. During hypnosis, patients are put into a relaxed, trance-like state by a hypnotherapist or through special hypnosis tapes. This state is not unlike that of meditation and visualization. However, unlike visualization where the patient imagines himself or herself relaxed and pain free, during hypnosis, the hypnotherapist uses the power of suggestion to help the patient relax, thereby reducing stress, headache pain, nausea, and vomiting. According to hypnotherapists, this is achieved through the subconscious mind, which controls every function of the body and is more open to suggestion than the conscious mind. Although scientists do not know why suggestions made while under hypnosis can reduce pain, hypnotherapy has become widely accepted as an effective complementary treatment. In fact, the College of Physicians and Surgeons at Columbia University in New York City offers a program on hypnosis to medical students and doctors.

A number of studies have been conducted on the effectiveness of hypnotism and headache pain. A 2002 study at Victoria University of Technology in Melbourne, Australia, for instance, had patients with migraine headaches keep a log for three months in

A patient participates in hypnosis therapy. Many studies demonstrate that hypnosis can reduce the frequency and severity of headaches.

which they recorded the frequency and severity of their headaches as well as the amount of medication they used. The patients continued keeping their daily logs for the next three months, during which time they also listened to headache-reduction hypnosis tapes. Then the data in the patients' logs were compared. Researchers found that during the three months in which the patients were hypnotized, they reported less frequent and less severe headaches. In addition, their medication use was cut in half. Based on this and other studies, many doctors endorse hypnotism as a complementary headache treatment. Headache expert and family physician Larry Deutsch of Ottawa, Canada, explains: "Hypnosis is effective . . . and provides a powerful complimentary or stand alone therapy to those who suffer from headaches. Stress reduction and relaxation techniques have an important role to play in the treatment in one of the most vexing problems physicians face in practice, the patient with headache."[37]

Biofeedback

Biofeedback is another method that trains the mind to control the body. Through biofeedback, people learn to regulate involuntary body functions such as muscle tension, blood flow, body temperature, and the workings of the nervous system. During a biofeedback session, headache patients wear special sensors on their head and scalp that electronically monitor their involuntary body functions. These sensors are connected to a computer and a monitor that provide the patient with immediate feedback. For example,

A patient receives biofeedback treatment. Biofeedback teaches patients to recognize when their muscles are tense and how to relax those muscles to alleviate headache pain.

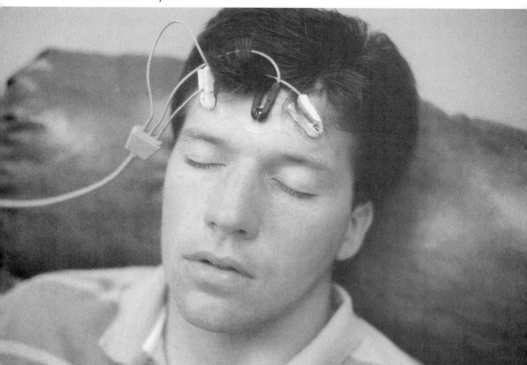

when patients are tensing the muscles in their forehead, which causes their blood vessels to constrict, the sensors send signals to the computer. These signals cause the computer to beep or lights to flash across the monitor. When patients see or hear these responses, they know that their muscles are tense. Patients can stop the responses by relaxing their muscles, which they learn to do through instructions from the biofeedback therapist.

Through this monitoring, people learn how their bodies feel when their muscles are tense and when they are relaxed as well as how to respond to tense muscles in order to relax them. Over time, they learn to carry out the same response when they are not connected to the biofeedback machine. This helps keep their blood vessels open. Indeed, biofeedback has been so effective in helping headache patients that the National Headache Foundation recommends it as a nonmedical treatment. Many patients and doctors agree. Medical doctor and headache sufferer Larry Dossey of Santa Fe, New Mexico, describes his experience: "I had classic migraines. . . . Nothing worked for it—and in desperation I learned how to do biofeedback, a form of relaxation training, which virtually solved the problem."[38]

Risks and Side Effects of Alternative Treatments

It is true that alternative treatments work for many headache patients. However, like conventional headache treatments, alternative treatments can pose health risks. Herbal treatments in particular can cause problems. Because herbs are natural, many people believe they are unconditionally safe. However, many herbs are as strong as drugs, and like drugs can cause a number of side effects. For example, feverfew can cause stomach pain, mouth ulcers, and swollen lips in some people, while ginseng's side effects include insomnia and diarrhea.

In addition, chemicals in herbs can interact with chemicals in drugs, causing dangerous consequences. According to the results of a study at the University of Utah in Salt Lake City reported at the 2003 annual scientific meeting of the American Headache Society, several popular herbal headache treatments, including ginseng and Saint-John's-wort, may interact with triptans and antidepressant medications in the liver. This can have toxic results when chemicals in the liver turn this combination into a poisonous, and potentially fatal, compound. In fact, it is illegal to sell Saint-John's-wort in France due to herb-drug interactions. In addition, these herbs and valerian root may actually cause or worsen headaches in some people. Even when patients do not mix herbal products and traditional medication, because of lack of set standards and regulations, some herbal products may be stronger than what is reported on their labels. This too can cause a bad reaction. For example, due to their anticoagulant properties, high doses of gingko biloba, ginseng, and Saint-John's-wort can inhibit the blood's ability to clot and cause dangerous bleeding.

Hands-on treatments can also cause problems. Cases of stroke have been reported after chiropractic manipulation of the neck. Although these cases are extremely rare, when the neck is manipulated and the head is rotated, these actions can cause blood vessels in the brain to burst or become stretched and blocked, causing a stroke. Complications from acupuncture treatment, such as the wounding of a nerve or blood vessel with an acupuncture needle, have been reported.

But despite these problems, through the use of alternative treatments, millions of headache patients find relief from headache pain while decreasing their dependence on headache medications. Consequently, many headache patients are willing to take the risk.

Chapter 4

Living with Headaches

PEOPLE WITH HEADACHES face a number of challenges. Clearly, the threat of a severe headache occurring at any time causes stress and anxiety. And when a headache does strike, it disturbs people's daily lives. Drew, a young headache sufferer, describes his experience: "I got two bad migraines this summer. The first was right before a big golf tournament. It was real important, but the headache threw me out of the tournament. The second was before an all-star game. I worked hard to make it to the all-stars. But I couldn't play."[39]

In an effort to avoid such disruptions and the accompanying anxiety and stress, many headache patients take steps to manage and thus control their headaches. In so doing, they lessen the severity and frequency of their headaches, which makes living with their condition easier.

Identifying Triggers

One of the first steps people with headaches take is identifying their personal headache triggers. This is often accomplished by keeping a headache diary. Such a diary is kept for about eight weeks. It is used to track headache attacks in order to determine what triggered them.

In a typical headache diary, patients record the date, time and duration, preceding symptoms, and intensity of headaches, the medicine they took and the dosage, and whether the medicine provided complete, moderate, or poor relief. In addition, patients list everything they ate and drank for twelve hours preceding the headache. They also track what activities they participated in, what their sleep schedule was like, what their stress level was, what environmental pollutants they came in contact with—including noises, odors, and bright lights—and for women, the date of their last menstrual period. After about eight weeks, patients and their doctors review the diaries, looking for any patterns. For example, if a patient notices that he or she often gets a headache after a stressful day at work or school, it becomes clear that stress is one of this individual's headache triggers. Similarly, if attacks coincide with the consumption of hot cocoa or fudge, the patient can deduce that chocolate is a trigger. Kathleen, who keeps a headache diary, explains what she hopes to gain:

Keeping a headache diary helps patients identify headache triggers.

I'm not sure what causes my headaches. My doctor asked me to keep a headache log. Whenever I get a headache, I have to write down what I've done activities-wise, and what I've eaten and drank for twelve hours before. Then I check the log after every headache to see if maybe I ate the same thing each time. I haven't found anything yet. But eventually, with the log, I think I'll be able to identify what's causing them.[40]

By keeping a headache diary and acting as a medical detective, patients can gain better control of their headaches. Once a pattern is identified and triggers are determined, patients can take steps to avoid or lessen their contact with their personal triggers. In some cases, this helps prevent headaches from occurring. Even if a person's triggers turn out to be unavoidable—such as air pollution, for example—by identifying specific triggers, patients can prepare to have abortive medicine handy when they must come in contact with these triggers. This will help to lessen the severity of a headache. In addition, keeping a headache diary can also help patients keep track of whether their headache medicine is working effectively. If it is not, they can tell their doctor, and a new medication, which may provide more relief, can be prescribed. Moreover, keeping track of medicine dosages can help patients to avoid overuse of medication and the rebound headaches that often result.

Indeed, keeping a headache diary is so useful that interested groups such as The Migraine Trust, a British headache information and support group, and Excedrin, an analgesic manufacturer, offer free copies of headache diaries on their websites. Headache patients are encouraged to print these headache diaries and use them to manage their headaches more effectively. Peterson explains:

> Keeping a migraine diary will help you take control of your life and better cope with your predisposition towards these menacing headaches. If you're not aware of your personal migraine triggers, this tool will help you—and your doctor—become more attuned. I recommend that all my patients keep one. Your migraine diary will enable you to track your own patterns and

be your own detective in determining what your headache triggers may be.[41]

Elimination Diet

For some people, keeping a headache diary is not enough, especially when it comes to identifying dietary headache triggers. In these people, rather than an individual food such as chocolate triggering their headaches, a combination of foods are responsible. Since food combinations can be endless, it is hard to determine these triggers through a headache diary alone. Some individuals may react to specific foods or food combinations only in certain quantities. Identifying what these combinations and quantities are can be tricky. Therefore, some patients combine the use of a headache diary with a headache trigger elimination diet.

Such a diet can be highly restricted. It involves the elimination of all likely headache triggers. For people who suspect they are sensitive to a wide variety of items, this includes caffeine, processed meats, chocolate, beans, aged cheeses, nuts, and alcoholic beverages. For other people, it may involve the elimination of only a few suspected triggers. Patients replace these foods with safe substitutes that are not commonly headache triggers, such as brown rice, chicken, fish, and vegetables. Then, in the course of one or two months, possible headache triggers are reintroduced into the patient's diet one at a time, in varying quantities and in different combinations, while patients carefully record their reactions in their headache diaries. In this manner, people learn how much of a possible trigger they can tolerate and whether or not the food affects them when eaten alone or only when combined with other possible triggers. Sharon, who thinks her son's headaches may be triggered by caffeine, talks about how she is using an elimination diet to identify his triggers:

> He loves soda, and that's what we think is causing his headaches. What else can it be? He has a simple life. He doesn't seem stressed, no big exams, no girlfriends yet. But he drinks a

lot of soda. We're trying to see if it might be the caffeine in the sodas. We made him stop drinking soda, and anything else with caffeine, like iced tea, and lattes; and we're gradually reintroducing it and seeing what happens. He's up to one cola a day. We'll keep increasing the amount and see what happens.[42]

Avoiding Food Triggers

Whether through the use of a headache diary alone or through the use of a headache diary combined with an elimination diet, once dietary and other headache triggers are identified, in order to lessen the frequency and severity of headaches, patients try to avoid these triggers. This is often easier said than done. Although avoiding dietary triggers, for instance, does not sound difficult, giving up a favorite food or drink is never easy. In order to compensate for the loss of a favorite food, headache patients find that substituting a safe alternative food in its place helps them to cope. For instance, many patients substitute cottage cheese for aged cheeses; and lamb, chicken, and fish for hot dogs and other processed meats. Similarly, they may opt for decaffeinated soda and coffee and fruit juice instead of wine, beer, and caffeinated beverages. Hard candy, cake, cookies, and Jell-O often are substituted for chocolate.

Although making these changes can be difficult, avoiding dietary triggers can really pay off. Paulino explains how avoiding red wine helped one of his patients:

> Jennifer . . . began experiencing recurrent headaches at the beginning of the summer following her twenty-third birthday. During that summer, she began dating a French exchange student from a well-to-do background. During their dates at high-priced French restaurants, Jennifer would drink red wine with her meals. Once the exact triggers were identified, Jennifer set about developing a plan for avoiding red wine. . . . Four months later, Jennifer's chronic headaches were reduced to an occasional, mild, nondescript head pain that occurred every three months on average.[43]

Changing Sleep Patterns

Like dietary triggers, irregular sleep patterns that trigger headaches can often be avoided. Such patterns include getting too much or not enough sleep as well as experiencing non-restorative sleep.

People may not get enough sleep because they stay up late to study, finish a project, or socialize. They may sleep late on the weekends in order to compensate for their lack of sleep. Unfortunately, this type of irregular sleep schedule appears to affect serotonin levels, triggering headaches in sensitive people. So, too, does having nonrestorative sleep. Such sleep is characterized by difficulty falling asleep or staying asleep. It is often interrupted by

Regulating sleep patterns helps sufferers control their headaches.

any number of things, such as a crying baby, street noises, or insomnia. Even though people who get nonrestorative sleep may spend six to eight hours in bed, as a result of sleep interruptions they report waking up feeling tired.

No matter what causes irregular sleep patterns, in order to combat and better control headaches, sensitive people must avoid them. According to headache experts Stafford and Jennifer Shoquist: "Dysfunctional [irregular] sleep looms as a pivotal lifestyle factor that you can change to get your body back into a positive groove and help avoid migraines."[44]

This is done by following a set sleep schedule that involves going to bed and waking up at the same time each day, no matter whether it is a weekday or weekend. Such a sleep schedule helps regulate an individual's sleep patterns, keeping sleep-triggered headaches at bay. In addition, patients plagued by nonrestorative sleep find that taking steps to make their sleep more restorative can help reduce their headaches. These steps include using tools to block out annoying sounds such as earplugs, soft background music, or a white-noise machine that produces a droning sound like the hum of an air conditioner. Patients also avoid activities right before bedtime that are known to keep people awake, such as exercising vigorously, drinking caffeinated beverages, or eating a large meal. Patients who make these changes report that they feel more refreshed upon awakening and experience fewer headaches.

Restricting Medication

Another common trigger, the overuse of headache medication, can also be managed. But this is not easy. It involves stopping the use of abortive medications for eight to twelve weeks. This can lead to patients' experiencing intense headache pain and, in the case of opiates, withdrawal symptoms. Therefore, most patients make this change under a doctor's supervision. Indeed, some patients check into a hospital or drug treatment facility while breaking the painkiller habit. Here issues of drug abuse are dealt with, and patients are helped to gradually discontinue painkilling medication in a step-by-step approach. This involves the offending drug being administered at smaller and smaller dosages until it is completely stopped. At the same time, other medications, such as preventive medicines, antidepressants, and steroids may be prescribed to help patients cope with rebound headaches until the pain cycle is broken. In addition, alternative treatments, such as biofeedback and relaxation therapy, may be used to help patients cope.

Of course, in order to better manage their headaches, once the symptoms of rebound headaches have ceased, patients must be careful not to overuse headache medication in the future.

Reducing Stress Through Exercise

Since many patients take abortive medication to cope with stress-triggered headaches, one way patients can avoid overusing headache medication is by managing stress. Even though it is impossible for people to eliminate all stress from their lives, people whose headaches are triggered by stress should avoid or lessen stress as much as possible. By doing this, they can reduce the frequency of stress-triggered headaches.

According to many patients and headache experts, one of the best ways to reduce stress is by participating in some form of moderate exercise. Although it is true that strenuous exercise can trigger headaches in some patients, moderate exercise usually does not. Since high-impact exercise appears to trigger headaches, exercise to alleviate stress-triggered headaches is usually low impact. Beneficial low-impact exercise includes walking, dancing, yoga, tai chi, bicycling, golfing, weight training, and swimming, to name just a few. Unlike strenuous exercise, moderate exercise does not affect blood sugar levels or stimulate the production of stress hormones. Instead, moderate exercise stimulates the brain to produce endorphins. Consequently, some people find that exercising at the start of a headache reduces headache pain. Debbie comments: "If I have a headache and I exercise, it helps a lot. Like tonight, I had a headache when I went to my exercise class. But after going and moving around for a half hour the headache got better and the pain was gone."[45]

Low-impact exercise like walking reduces stress and helps to prevent headache pain.

Exercise also strengthens the body, and improves blood flow and the exerciser's general health. Since healthier people are better equipped to handle any type of pain, exercisers can cope more easily with headaches. Moreover, stronger muscles translate to less strain on the muscles that support the head. This reduces the possibility of muscle tenderness in the neck and shoulders, which can cause muscle contractions that may lead to decreased blood flow and headaches.

In addition, regular exercise is known to improve sleep, a benefit for people who suffer from sleep-triggered headaches. In fact, regular, moderate exercise of at least three times a week for about thirty minutes a session appears to prevent headaches from occurring. Experts theorize this may be the result of improved blood circulation.

Staying Active

Staying active, whether through moderate exercise, by having fun with friends and family, or participating in a hobby, also lessens stress and stress-triggered headaches. Many headache patients find that keeping busy doing things they enjoy takes their mind off stressful thoughts and relaxes them. Hobbies such as reading, painting, music, sewing, quilting, and writing are just a few activities headache patients say help them to relax, as do social activities like scouts, moviegoing, school clubs, and visiting with friends and family. Debbie, who stays active in order to cope with stress and stress-induced headaches, explains: "I have to control stress to control my headaches. I try to keep myself from stressing. I read or go to a movie to mellow out. That way I am in control."[46]

Lifestyle Modifications

Unlike stress, other headache triggers, such as bright lights, noise, certain smells, and air pollutants, are harder to control. However, once they are identified, people with these triggers often make changes in their lifestyles in an effort to limit their exposure to them. For some people, this involves avoiding certain activities. For instance, when loud noise triggers headaches, people may avoid attending concerts in large arenas or sporting events where there is a lot of noise. Instead they may watch sports events on television where they can control the sound and listen to music at home or attend concerts in small, quiet venues where they make sure not to sit close to the speakers. When loud noises cannot be avoided, some headache patients wear earplugs, or earphones connected to a portable CD player playing soft music in order to muffle the noise.

Similarly, people whose headaches are triggered by bright or flickering lights often avoid driving at night when bright car headlights can trigger a headache. They may also avoid taking a ski or beach vacation, since sunlight reflecting off snow, sand, or water is glaring and can trigger headaches. When bright light cannot be avoided, these people carry sunglasses with them everywhere and use them when exposed to bright light, either outdoors or indoors.

In the same manner, people whose headaches are triggered by certain odors modify their lifestyles to limit their exposure to these odors. For instance, people who are sensitive to certain perfumes avoid buying magazines with perfume samples or going to department stores where perfume is sprayed into the air. They may also ask friends and loved ones not to wear perfume when they are present and often use scent-free beauty products themselves. A woman talks about the changes she made: "I got rid of products that were scented and even changed to detergent and soaps free of perfumes. These things made a big difference—I rarely get a headache anymore."[47]

Likewise, people whose headaches are triggered by the smell of a wood fire report avoiding camping trips and any social event that involves a fireside gathering. At home, these people often use a gas log in place of a traditional fire. When smoke itself is a headache trigger, headache patients try to avoid being around people who smoke. This often involves avoiding smoky places such as bars. In some cases, it may mean avoiding certain friends, coworkers, and family members when they are smoking. Peterson explains: "Passive smoke inhalation can also be a major headache trigger. If you live with a smoker who can't or won't

Ways to Manage Headaches

- **Keep a headache diary**
- **Avoid triggers**
- **Get regular sleep**
- **Eat a healthy diet**
- **Get moderate exercise**
- **Reduce stress**
- **Restrict medication**

Smoking is a common headache trigger. Avoiding exposure to cigarette smoke can help prevent headaches.

quit set some guidelines to protect your health. Ask that person to smoke outside your home or in closed, designated areas in the house, which you can avoid."[48] Moreover, since smoking tobacco can constrict blood vessels, which can encourage the development of headaches, patients who smoke are advised to quit.

When indoor pollutants trigger headaches, patients make an effort to limit their exposure to them. If the culprits are strong chemicals in cleaning fluids, many people switch to natural cleaning agents like vinegar and water. When people cannot avoid strong chemicals, they find that opening a window or going outside often helps them to cope, as does wearing a special mask similar to a surgical mask that filters out chemicals in the air. Some people even wear a mask outdoors to limit their exposure to air pollution.

Talking to a Professional

Even when people make lifestyle changes and limit their exposure to headache triggers, many headache patients are still plagued by anxiety over when a headache may strike. Such anxiety stresses the body and can trigger headaches. In order to avoid this, these individuals often find that talking to a counselor, psychologist, or psychiatrist helps them to cope. Through counseling sessions, patients learn how to deal with their fears. Counselors help patients develop a preparedness plan that lessens their dread of a headache striking. Such a plan often includes simple things like being sure to always have abortive medicine handy or taking time out and relaxing when they feel tired or anxious. In addition, counselors often instruct patients in specific coping skills, such as relaxation therapy, that help them deal with their anxiety. Moreover, a psychiatrist may prescribe medication that helps individuals better handle stress. Indeed, many headache patients report that seeing a mental health professional helps them to take a more positive and active role in dealing with their headaches.

Coping with an Attack

Despite the many steps headache sufferers take to better manage their headaches, sometimes a headache will strike. When this occurs, many people have a set procedure that helps them to cope. Since taking abortive medicine at the first sign of a headache seems to provide the most effective relief, headache sufferers carry their medicine with them wherever they go in order to have it handy whenever they need it. Sharon, the mother who thinks her son's headaches may be triggered by caffeine, also has a daughter who gets migraines. Sharon explains, "She keeps Imitrex in her purse with her all the time, and takes it the minute she has symptoms."[49]

Then most headache sufferers try to stop what they are doing and rest until their medicine takes effect. Some people have developed individual strategies that help lessen the intensity of their headaches. For instance, some find that after taking medicine, taking a warm bath or bathing their forehead with warm water helps lessen their headache pain. This is usually followed by lying down in a dark, quiet room. When possible, patients try to sleep. Often when they awaken, their headache is gone. Dina explains her strategy: "I take a warm shower or bath. I think the warm water gets the blood circulating through my body, and reduces the pressure in my head. I also just soak my feet in warm water. I don't know why, but it seems to help."[50]

It is evident that living with headaches can be difficult. But when headache patients take steps to help manage their headaches, they experience less frequent and less painful headaches. And even when headaches do strike, these individuals are better able to deal with them. As a result, headache patients can live active and fulfilling lives.

Chapter 5

What the Future Holds

HEADACHE RESEARCH IS focused on learning what factors cause or encourage the development of headaches. Since certain dietary, sleep-related, and emotional factors are involved in the workings of blood vessels and the flow of blood to the brain, scientists are focusing their attention on investigating the link between these factors and headaches. If such factors can be identified, scientists can then develop ways to rectify them and thus prevent headaches. At the same time, scientists are working on developing more advanced methods to manage headaches.

A Nutritional Deficiency

Scientists know that the body needs certain nutrients in order for blood vessels to work effectively. These nutrients include magnesium and riboflavin. Since headaches are linked to blood-flow changes in the brain, scientists theorize that a deficiency in either of these nutrients may cause problems in the workings of blood vessels, resulting in headaches. Therefore, a number of studies are being conducted exploring this theory.

Magnesium

One of the most widely studied nutrients is magnesium. Scientists say that magnesium has an antivasospastic action on blood vessels: That is, it keeps the arteries from going into spasms. It also inhibits the constriction and dilation of blood vessels. Magnesium is also thought to be essential in keeping hormones balanced, which helps prevent hormonally triggered headaches.

Scientists believe that magnesium regulates muscle tone throughout the body, thus alleviating muscle tension that can lead to headaches. They also think that magnesium may be involved in the regulation and transmission of serotonin. Therefore, they theorize that when people lack an adequate supply of magnesium, they are more likely to develop headaches. In fact, some studies have shown that many headache patients have lower-than-normal levels of magnesium.

A 2002 study at the University of Pecs, Hungary, for example, examined magnesium levels in people with migraines. In this study, during a twenty-four-hour period, three thousand milligrams of magnesium was given to forty subjects, half of whom were migraine sufferers and half of whom were not. Baseline samples of the subjects' blood and urine were taken at the start of the study and after dosing. At the start, both groups had similar levels of magnesium in their bloodstream. The migraine group, however, had less magnesium in their urine. At the end of

Some scientists believe that inadequate amounts of magnesium in the body can trigger headaches.

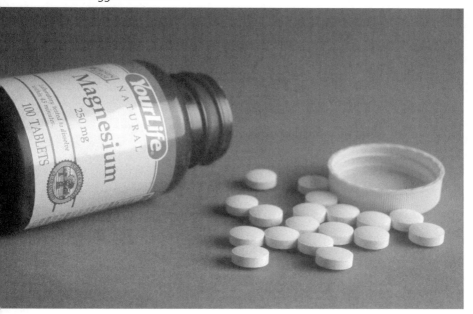

the study, both groups had significantly higher levels of magnesium in their blood, and the control group also had high levels of magnesium in their urine. The magnesium level in the urine of the migraine group, on the other hand, was still low. This is important because magnesium is water soluble. This means that excess magnesium is not stored in the body. Instead, after the body uses all the magnesium it needs, excess magnesium is eliminated from the body in urine. The researchers concluded that the migraine group retained the magnesium in order to normalize low magnesium levels in their bodies, suggesting a magnesium deficiency in these subjects.

Dr. Alexander Mauskop, a leading expert in the relationship between magnesium and headaches, estimates that as many as 50 percent of all migraine patients and 40 percent of all cluster headache patients may be deficient in magnesium. One study led by Mauskop and conducted at the State University of New York Downstate Medical Center in Brooklyn in 2002 looked at the link between a magnesium deficiency and hormonally triggered headaches. In this study, researchers analyzed magnesium levels in blood samples of sixty-one women with menstrual-associated migraines. Forty-five percent of the subjects had low magnesium levels. "The high incidence of ionized magnesium deficiency we found in our patients during menstrual migraine attacks indicates that magnesium may have a role in the development of the disease in a subgroup of patients,"[51] explains Mauskop.

Based on the results of these and other studies, researchers are exploring whether treatment with magnesium can prevent or lessen both hormonally triggered and nonhormonally triggered headaches. To test whether magnesium can prevent headaches, a 1996 study at the Munich-Harlaching Clinic in Germany divided eighty-one migraine patients into two groups. One group received six hundred milligrams of magnesium everyday for twelve weeks, while the other received a placebo. The frequency of headache attacks in both groups was monitored and compared. Headaches in the group taking magnesium were reduced by 41 percent compared to the placebo group whose headaches decreased by 15 percent. In addition, the duration and intensity of only the magnesium group's headaches decreased.

With such encouraging results, it is not surprising that interest in the role magnesium plays in headaches is growing. If scientists can conclusively prove that people who suffer from chronic headaches are deficient in magnesium, then it may be possible to supplement headache sufferers' diets with large doses of magnesium in order to prevent headaches. However, since large doses of magnesium can cause stomach upset and diarrhea, scientists want to continue studying the link between headaches and magnesium before prescribing the mineral. Nonetheless, many doctors are advising headache patients to add magnesium-rich foods, such as leafy green vegetables, whole grain cereal and breads, seafood, milk, and bananas, to their diets.

Riboflavin

Riboflavin, or vitamin B2, is another nutrient that scientists are investigating. Riboflavin, which is found in whole grains, organ meats, mushrooms, and leafy green vegetables, is required for cells to efficiently use oxygen. Scientists know that before a headache strikes, the brain's supply of oxygen is reduced. Having adequate riboflavin helps people to efficiently utilize even reduced amounts of oxygen. Conversely, without adequate riboflavin, the body has trouble metabolizing oxygen and needs increased rather than decreased oxygen in order to function normally. Therefore, scientists theorize that a combination of reduced oxygen and riboflavin causes headaches. Correspondingly, if headache patients take large doses of riboflavin, their brains will be able to use oxygen more efficiently thus preventing headaches.

To test this theory, in 1998, researchers at the University of Liege in Belgium gave fifty-five migraine patients four hundred milligrams of riboflavin daily for three months, while a control group was given a placebo. The subjects kept a headache diary in which they recorded the number of migraines they had during this time and the severity and duration of each attack. Fifty-nine percent of the patients in the riboflavin group had at least a 50

Leafy green vegetables are a good source of riboflavin. Studies suggest that a deficiency of riboflavin can cause headaches.

percent reduction in the number of headaches they experienced, whereas only 15 percent of the placebo group noted any improvement. The researchers observed that the longer the subjects took riboflavin, the more effective it became. This led them to speculate that headache patients may be so deficient in riboflavin that it must build up in their systems before it can work. Therefore, scientists plan to conduct a long-term study to see whether the effectiveness of riboflavin increases with time. If so, treating people prone to headaches with daily doses of riboflavin may prevent headaches.

In the meantime, many headache sufferers and doctors are experimenting with riboflavin supplements. One such headache sufferer explains: "I found it took about a month to kick in, but after that it seemed to work in conjunction with my preventive meds. I notice a big difference without it."[52]

Too Much Dietary Fat

Another group of scientists thinks that too much dietary fat, rather than a deficiency of certain nutrients, affects the workings of blood vessels and causes headaches. Scientists know that high levels of fat in the bloodstream thicken the blood and slow down blood flow. When the blood is too thick, it becomes difficult for platelets to move easily. As a result, the platelets clump together, which, many experts say, causes a number of other biochemical changes that lead to headaches. In addition, a number of unrelated headache triggers are also linked to a rise in blood fat. Stress and hunger, for instance, cause the body to release stored fat into the bloodstream for energy to help the body cope with danger or hunger. Alcohol and caffeine also appear to raise blood fat levels, as do hormonal changes. Therefore, some scientists hypothesize that high blood fat is the cause of headaches.

Curious about the possible link between high blood fat and headaches, between 1994 and 1996 scientists at Loma Linda University, California, conducted a study to see whether reducing migraine patients' blood-fat levels would prevent headaches. The study was conducted over a twelve-week period. The first month was the control month. During this time, the subjects maintained their normal eating habits and kept detailed headache diaries. At the end of the first month, the subjects' blood fat, in the form of blood cholesterol, was measured. For the next two months, the subjects were instructed to reduce their fat consumption to no more than 30 grams a day and to continue keeping their headache diaries. Since some of the subjects normally ate as much as 120 grams of fat each day, this was a reduction of approximately 75 percent. At the end of the twelve weeks, the subjects' blood was again tested and their headache diaries evaluated.

According to Zuzana Bic, director of the study, "The outcome of the experiment surpassed even the most optimistic expectations. It has demonstrated clearly a very strong connection between high dietary fat intake and migraine headache. Patients who had decreased their fat intake significantly lowered their frequency, intensity, and duration of migraine headaches."[53]

Indeed, before reducing their fat intake, the subjects averaged nine headaches per month. At the end of the study, this was reduced to an average of two headaches per month, an improvement of 71 percent. In addition, based on a rating scale from zero to five with zero indicating no pain and five indicating extreme pain, the intensity of the subjects' headaches fell from an average of three to below one, a decrease of about 66 percent. Similarly, the duration of the subjects' headaches decreased by 74 percent while blood fat or cholesterol levels decreased from an average of 206 to 178.

Although more studies must be conducted in order to confirm that high blood fat causes headaches and that a diet low in fat can prevent them, it is an interesting theory. Some scientists, including Bic, are encouraging their patients to make lifestyle changes that include reducing dietary fat and increasing fat-burning physical activity as a way to prevent headaches. Bic explains, "One of the most important contributions of the study was the identification of elevated amounts of blood fat as a common denominator of primary headaches. . . . This opened the way to a radically new treatment of headaches based on specific lifestyle modifications to reduce blood-fat levels."[54]

Eating a healthy, low-fat diet and increasing fat-burning physical activity can help headache sufferers reduce the frequency of their headaches.

Most health experts agree that limiting one's fat consumption is a good general health practice. Therefore, following Bic's advice should, at the very least, help headache patients to improve their overall health, which should help them better cope with headaches.

Poor Digestion and Headaches

Other scientists think that poor digestion, which hinders the way the body utilizes nutrients, rather than a deficiency or an overabundance of certain nutrients causes headaches. These scientists theorize that people with headaches cannot efficiently digest nutrients or effectively eliminate waste. This keeps essential nutrients from reaching the brain as well as causing toxins, which are not eliminated through bowel movements, to build up in the bloodstream and thus cause headaches. These scientists speculate that if these two factors can be corrected, then headaches can be prevented. Therefore, in 2001, a group of naturopathic physicians in Hamden, Connecticut; Schuylkill Haven, Pennsylvania; and Orem, Utah, recruited forty migraine patients to determine the validity of this theory. For ninety days, all the patients were administered specially formulated supplements designed to improve digestion and elimination. The first supplement, known as Combination A, consisted of helpful bacteria known to stimulate digestion and the absorption of nutrients, and peptides that are natural substances commonly used to improve digestion in patients with intestinal and stomach injuries. The second supplement, called Combination B, was made up of twenty-one different ingredients, including a variety of vitamins, minerals, herbs, fibers, and natural chemicals.

After ninety days, in which the subjects took three capsules of Combination A and two capsules of Combination B ten minutes before their two largest meals of the day, 60 percent of the subjects experienced almost total relief from migraine attacks. According to the researchers, "These study results support the theory that migraines may be, at least in part, caused by an underlying deterioration of normal body functioning. In this study by improving assimilation [digestion] and elimination mechanisms, the manifestation of migraines diminished or ceased for the majority of the participants."[55]

Although the results were encouraging, the study did not include a control group. Therefore, a larger study in a medical hospital with a control group is being planned. Still, it cannot hurt migraine patients to consume foods that stimulate the digestion and elimination process, such as fiber-rich food like bran, fruits, and vegetables, as well as yogurt that contains beneficial bacteria. Besides being healthy, based on the result of the study, these foods may help prevent headaches.

Sleep Issues

While some scientists are examining dietary factors, others are investigating the possibility that the sleep disorder sleep apnea may cause headaches. People with sleep apnea stop breathing while they are sleeping for periods of at least ten seconds at a time. Since this reduces the supply of oxygen to the brain, scientists are exploring a possible link to headaches. Because cluster headaches most often begin while a person is sleeping, scientists are focusing their attention on the connection between sleep apnea and cluster headaches.

In 2000, scientists at the Sleep Disorders Center at the University of Michigan in Ann Arbor measured the breathing patterns of twenty-five cluster headache patients while the subjects slept. Of these, 80 percent were found to have obstructed breathing. The more severe the sleep apnea, the more likely the subject would awaken with a cluster headache. Consequently, the scientists concluded that sleep-disordered breathing is likely to occur in cluster headache patients.

Hence, treating sleep apnea may help prevent cluster headaches. In fact, in a case study reported by the Organization for Understanding Cluster Headaches, doctors at the University of Manitoba, Section of Respiratory Diseases, in Winnipeg, Canada, found that treating a cluster headache patient for sleep apnea eliminated the patient's headaches entirely.

In a similar manner, since snoring is caused by a breathing disturbance, scientists hypothesize that snoring, too, may be linked

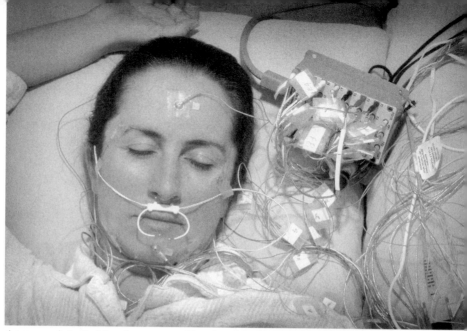

A woman is tested for sleep apnea. Treating this disorder may help prevent the onset of cluster headaches.

to headaches. A 2003 study at the National Institutes of Health in Bethesda, Maryland, for example, compared the snoring habits of 206 people with chronic headaches to 507 people with occasional headaches. The study found that the chronic headache patients were 2.5 times more likely to be nightly snorers than the control group. Scientists do not know whether snoring causes headaches or vice versa. But they do believe there is a link between the two, and future studies are planned. In the meantime, some doctors are assessing and treating headache patients for snoring in hopes of preventing headaches.

Suppressed Anger

Other headache specialists wonder if emotional issues take a physical toll on blood vessels and cause headaches. Researchers at Saint Louis University in Missouri studied 422 people, 171 of whom suffered from chronic headaches and 251 who did not. Looking for a common emotional link, the researchers found that most of the headache sufferers all dealt with anger by bottling it up inside. The headache-free group, on the other hand, handled anger by letting it out. Scientists know that suppressing anger stresses the body and contributes to other diseases in which blood flow and blood vessels malfunction, such as heart disease, ulcers, and high blood pressure. Suppressing anger, they theorize, causes people to tense their muscles, which in turn tenses blood vessels, in response. Anger also causes the body to respond by releasing a constant supply of stress hormones to cope with the anger. Both are factors that can result in headaches. Commenting on the findings of the study, Dr. Merle Diamond, associate director of the Diamond Headache Clinic in Chicago, explains: "Just like some people get ulcers and grind their teeth, some people get headaches. Anger has to come out somewhere."[56]

Researchers do not know if every headache patient suppresses feelings of anger. If, through other studies, they find this to be the case, then psychiatric treatment that deals with handling anger might become the norm for headache sufferers. For now, Diamond suggests that in an effort to prevent headaches, people develop methods to cope with suppressed anger, such as practicing martial arts.

Botox Treatment

While some scientists are trying to determine what causes headaches, others are developing new forms of treatment. One such treatment is the botulinum toxin, a bacteria commonly known as Botox. Used to alleviate facial wrinkles, when Botox is injected into the face, it temporarily paralyzes facial muscles. Surprisingly, a number of headache patients undergoing Botox wrinkle treatment have reported that the substance also alleviated their headaches. Although scientists do not know why Botox has an effect on headaches, this coincidence prompted a number of studies investigating the feasibility of using Botox as a preventive headache treatment. So far, the results have been promising.

The largest study to date was conducted in 2003 in San Diego, California, by Kaiser Permanente, a nonprofit health maintenance company that sponsors research on different health care issues. In this study, 271 migraine- and tension-headache patients received preventive treatment of two to five Botox injections every three months. As a result, 80 percent of the subjects reported that their headaches were less frequent, less intense, or both, and 60 percent reported getting good to excellent pain relief. Since three-quarters of the subjects had previously tried many different pain remedies without success, these statistics were encouraging. In addition, unlike many of the subjects' experiences with headache medications, 95 percent reported no side effects with Botox. According to the director of the study, neurologist Andrew M. Blumenfeld, "Many of these patients otherwise would be left with narcotics as their best option. Our study also shows Botox causes fewer side effects than many standard medications."[57]

Although the FDA has not yet approved Botox for headache treatment, because of the mounting evidence of its effectiveness,

A woman receives a Botox injection. Scientists are currently researching Botox as a preventative treatment for headaches.

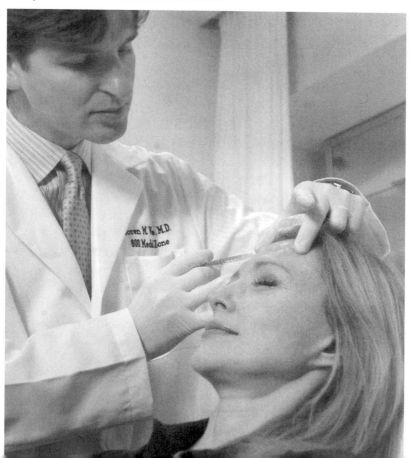

many experts think it will be approved soon. In fact, because it is approved as a treatment for wrinkles, some headache patients are already using it as a dual treatment. A patient who was administered twenty-two Botox injections explains: "I felt a difference almost immediately. My headaches are less severe, and I've cut back on other medications."[58]

Electrode Implants

Even though Botox appears to be effective in treating most migraine and tension headaches, it is not powerful enough to relieve the intense pain of cluster headaches. These stubborn headaches need a stronger form of treatment. Therefore, scientists are exploring a powerful pain treatment that has long been used to alleviate back pain. This treatment involves implanting a tiny electrical device on a nerve, such as the one above the eye for cluster headaches. The device, which the patients turn on or off via a remote control, emits an electrical signal to the nerve and subsequently disrupts pain signals.

Although such a device has been implanted into people's spinal cords to treat back pain, it was first used for headaches in 2003 when doctors at Rush-Presbyterian-St. Luke's Medical Center and Northwestern Memorial Hospital, both in Chicago, implanted a device into six headache patients with excellent results. Theresa, one patient, explains: "The minute he put it in, the pain was gone."[59]

Treatment with electrical implants is still experimental, however. Scientists are investigating whether the device can be implanted in the scalp or forehead to treat severe migraine headaches as well as developing even smaller devices. Indeed, scientists are working hard to perfect this form of treatment, just as they are doing with Botox. It is hoped that in the not-too-distant future, these treatments will provide much-needed relief for chronic headache pain. At the same time, there is optimism in the scientific community that eventually the cause of headaches will be determined. With that discovery, a way to permanently prevent headaches will be found. Therefore, headache patients can look to the future with hope.

Notes

Introduction: Headaches—A Costly Complaint

1. Quoted in Migraine Association of Ireland, "Teenagers," www.migraine.ie.
2. Quoted in Diane Stafford and Jennifer Shoquist, *Migraines for Dummies*. New York: Wiley Publishing, 2003, p. 222.
3. Quoted in Christina Peterson, *The Women's Migraine Survival Guide*. New York: A Harper Resource Book, 1999, p. 4.

Chapter 1: What Is a Headache?

4. Debbie, interview with the author, Las Cruces, NM, August 5, 2003.
5. Joel Paulino and Ceabert J. Griffith, *The Headache Sourcebook.* Chicago: Contemporary Books, 2001, p. 58.
6. Quoted in Peterson, *The Women's Migraine Survival Guide*, p. 4.
7. Dina, interview with the author, Las Cruces, NM, July 25, 2003.
8. Quoted in ABC Online-Australian Broadcasting Commission, "Radio National the Health Report, Cluster Headaches," August 9, 1999. www.abc.net.au.
9. Quoted in ABC Online, "Radio National the Health Report, Cluster Headaches."
10. Debbie, interview with the author.
11. Peterson, *The Women's Migraine Survival Guide*, p. 78.
12. Cindy, interview with the author, Las Cruces, NM, July 24, 2003.
13. Debbie, interview with the author.
14. Cindy, interview with the author.
15. Quoted in Peterson, *The Women's Migraine Survival Guide*, p. 5.

Chapter 2: Diagnosis and Treatment

16. Quoted in Cluster Headaches.com, "Cluster Headaches," www.clusterheadaches.com.
17. Quoted in Peterson, *The Women's Migraine Survival Guide*, p. 10.
18. Drew, interview with the author, El Paso, TX, August 24, 2003.
19. Quoted in Peterson, *The Women's Migraine Survival Guide*, p. 13.
20. Stafford and Shoquist, *Migraines for Dummies*, p. 99.
21. Debbie, interview with the author.
22. Quoted in Peterson, *The Women's Migraine Survival Guide*, p. 139.
23. Quoted in Peterson, *The Women's Migraine Survival Guide*, p. 145.
24. Nita, interview with the author, Mesquite, NM, July 29, 2003.
25. Elizabeth Connell Henderson, *Understanding Addiction.* Jackson: University of Mississippi, 2000, p. 63.
26. Quoted in National Headache Foundation, "Over the Counter Pain Medication May Cause Headaches," www.headaches.org.
27. Quoted in Stafford and Shoquist, *Migraines for Dummies*, p. 59.

Chapter 3: Alternative Treatments

28. Debbie, interview with the author.
29. Peterson, *The Women's Migraine Survival Guide*, p. 152.
30. Steven Foster Group, "Ginger," www.herbphoto.com.
31. Lam Kam Sang Medical Research Institute, "Heklin," www.lamkamsang.com.
32. Peterson, *The Women's Migraine Survival Guide*, p. 154.
33. Quoted in Harmonious Healthcare, "Testimonials," www.harmonioushealthcare.co.uk.
34. Quoted in Acupuncture Information, "Testimonials," www.seattleacupuncture.com.
35. Quoted in Peterson, *The Women's Migraine Survival Guide*, p. 159.
36. Paulino and Griffith, *The Headache Sourcebook*, p. 184.
37. Larry Deutsch, Cancer Treatment Research Foundation,

"Headache, Hypnosis, and Stress: A Case History," ctrf. healthology.com.

38. Quoted in *Delicious Living*, "A Conversation with Larry Dossey, MD," Annual Guide 2003, p. 58.

Chapter 4: Living with Headaches

39. Drew, interview with the author.
40. Kathleen, interview with the author, El Paso, TX, August 24, 2003.
41. Peterson, *The Women's Migraine Survival Guide*, p. 69.
42. Sharon, interview with the author, El Paso, TX, August 24, 2003.
43. Paulino and Griffith, *The Headache Sourcebook*, p. 47.
44. Stafford and Shoquist, *Migraines for Dummies*, p. 181.
45. Debbie, interview with the author.
46. Debbie, interview with the author.
47. Quoted in Stafford and Shoquist, *Migraines for Dummies*, p. 176.
48. Peterson, *The Women's Migraine Survival Guide*, p. 79.
49. Sharon, interview with the author.
50. Dina, interview with the author.

Chapter 5: What the Future Holds

51. Quoted in World Headache Alliance, "Magnesium Deficiency Linked to Menstrual Migraines in Some Women," www.w-h-a.org.
52. Quoted in RemedyFind, "Vitamin B-2 (Riboflavin)," www.remedyfind.com.
53. Zuzana Bic and L. Francis Bic, *No More Headaches No More Migraines*, New York: Avery, 1999, p. 40.
54. Bic and Bic, *No More Headaches No More Migraines*, p. 43.
55. James Sensenig, Jeffrey Marrongelle, Mark Johnson, and Thomas Staverosky, "Treatment of Migraine with Targeted Nutrition Focused on Improved Assimilation and Elimination," *Alternative Medicine Review*, 6, no. 5, 2001, p. 493.
56. Quoted in Elena Conis, "Suppressed Anger Linked to Headaches," *Albuquerque Journal*, July 28, 2003, p. C1.
57. Quoted in American Headache Society, "Botox Relieves

Headaches with Few Side Effects, Suggests Largest Study Yet," www.ahsnet.org.

58. Quoted in Peg Rosen, "The Pain Truth," *Good Housekeeping*, May 2003, p. 86.

59. Quoted in "Electrode Implants Zap Some Types of Headaches," *Dallas Morning News*, February 18, 2003, p. 4A.

Glossary

abortive medicine: Medicine taken to treat the symptoms of a headache.

adrenal: A stress hormone.

analgesics: Painkilling medicines.

anticonvulsants: Medications used to treat seizures and also used to prevent headaches.

antidepressants: Medications used to treat depression and also used to prevent headaches.

antivasospastic action: An action that prevents arteries from going into a spasm, as well as inhibiting the constriction and dilation of blood vessels that leads to headaches.

aura: A visual disturbance that occurs before a migraine attack in some patients.

Ayurveda: Traditional Indian medicine.

beta blockers: A medication used to aid in headache prevention.

calcium channel blockers: A medication used to aid headache prevention.

chronic headaches: Headaches that recur at least three times a month over a period of months or years.

cluster headaches: An extremely painful type of primary headaches. These headaches occur in quick succession.

cortisol: A stress hormone.

endorphin: A natural chemical produced by the brain that lessens feelings of pain and gives a feeling of well-being.

episodic headaches: Headaches that occur occasionally.

estrogen: A female sex hormone.

feverfew: An herb used to treat headaches and heart disease.

hormones: A variety of chemicals produced by the body to regulate different bodily functions.

migraine headache: The second most common form of primary headaches and one of the most painful and debilitating.

neurologist: A medical doctor who specializes in diseases involving the brain and nervous system.

neurotransmitter: A chemical messenger that carries signals from the brain throughout the body.

opiates: Powerful pain-killing medication derived from opium.

placebo: An ineffective medicine, such as a sugar pill, that is often used as a control in scientific research.

platelets: A type of red blood cell.

preventive medicine: A medicine taken to prevent diseases and illnesses.

primary headache: A headache not caused by another medical condition.

secondary headache: A headache caused by another medical condition.

serotonin: A neurotransmitter involved in carrying messages concerning pain, the workings of blood vessels, sleep, and mood.

tension headaches: A mild type of primary headaches that cause a squeezing pain in the head.

triptans: A family of drugs used to treat headache symptoms.

vasoconstriction: Narrowing of a blood vessel.

vasodilation: Widening (dilating) of a blood vessel.

Organizations to Contact

American Council for Headache Education
19 Mantua Road
Mt. Royal, NJ 08061
(856) 423-0258
www.achenet.org

This organization offers information and support for headache patients and their families, as well as information on clinical trials and the latest headache research.

American Headache Society
19 Mantua Road
Mt. Royal, NJ 08061
(856) 423-0043
www.ahsnet.org
ahshq@talley.com

A professional organization for people interested in the study and treatment of headaches. It provides information on the latest headache research and publishes a scientific journal on headaches.

M.A.G.N.U.M.
Migraine Awareness Group:
A National Understanding for Migraineurs
113 S. Saint Asaph, Suite 300
Alexandria, VA 22314
(703) 739-9384
www.migraines.org

Offers information on every aspect of migraines, including lists of doctors and clinics throughout the United States who specialize in treating migraines, tips on coping with migraines, and migraine treatment and management.

National Headache Foundation
820 North Orleans, Suite 217
Chicago, IL 60610
(888) NHF-5552
www.headaches.org

Offers a wealth of educational resources on every aspect of headaches for patients and doctors. In addition, this organization sponsors clinical trials and special events and programs to support headache patients. The website also offers a number of helpful links.

World Headache Alliance
3288 Old Coach Road
Burlington, Ontario, Canada L7N3P7
www.w-h-a.org

This international organization, based in Canada, offers information on every type of headache, polls and surveys, suggested reading lists, headache news, and international events.

For Further Reading

Books

American College of Physicians, *Migraines and Other Headaches.* London: Dorling Kindersley, 2000. A colorful guide to headaches that looks at the varieties and causes of headaches, as well as headaches in women and children.

David Buchholz, *Heal Your Headache.* New York: Workman Publishing, 2002. Discusses what headaches are and how to use diet to control them.

Dennis Fox and Jeanne Rejaunier, *The Complete Idiot's Guide to Migraines and Other Headaches.* Indianapolis: Alpha Books, 2000. A concise and easy-to-read book that covers headache causes, treatment, and management in an entertaining manner.

Websites

About Headaches (www.headaches.about.com). The latest news in headaches, as well as articles on managing the disease, rebound headaches, and success stories.

Excedrin Headache Resource Center (www.excedrin.com). This pain-relief manufacturer offers advice on how to better manage headaches, as well as providing questions and answers about headaches.

Headache Net (www.headache.net). Offers live webcasts, an overview of headaches, information on headache types and treatment, and ways to deal with rebound headaches.

Migraine Trust (www.migrainetrust.org). A British organization that offers free headache diaries, provides information and support, as well as answering headache questions through an e-mail link on the website.

New York Headache Center (www.nyheadache.com). Offers information and recent magazine and news articles about headaches.

O.U.C.H. Organization for Understanding Cluster Headaches (www.clusterheadaches.org). Provides a wealth of information and support on every aspect of cluster headaches.

Migraine Relief Center (www.migrainehelp.com). Sponsored by the manufacturer of the headache drug Imitrex, this website provides information on the causes, symptoms, triggers, and impact of migraines. It also offers questions and answers.

Steven Foster Group (www.herbphoto.com). Offers photographs and a discussion on the medicinal uses of a wide variety of herbs.

Works Consulted

Books

Zuzana Bic and L. Francis Bic, *No More Headaches No More Migraines.* New York: Avery, 1999. This book focuses on the link between a high-fat diet and headaches and on the theory that making dietary changes can eliminate headaches.

Elizabeth Connell Henderson, *Understanding Addiction.* Jackson: University of Mississippi, 2000. Although not about headaches, this book discusses the problems of addiction to pain pills, a frequent problem for headache patients.

Joel Paulino and Ceabert J. Griffith, *The Headache Sourcebook.* Chicago: Contemporary Books, 2001. A detailed book that deals with the symptoms, treatment, and triggers of all types of headaches.

Christina Peterson, *The Women's Migraine Survival Guide.* New York: A Harper Resource Book, 1999. The cause and treatment of migraine headaches are specifically examined as they relate to women.

Diane Stafford and Jennifer Shoquist, *Migraines for Dummies.* New York: Wiley Publishing, 2003. An easy-to-read book that deals with every aspect of headaches.

Periodicals

Elena Conis, "Suppressed Anger Linked to Headaches," *Albuquerque Journal,* July 28, 2003.

Dallas Morning News, "Electrode Implants Zap Some Types of Headaches," February 18, 2003.

Delicious Living, "A Conversation with Larry Dossey, MD," Annual Guide 2003.

V. Miller, T. Palermo, S. Powers, M. Scher, and A. Hershey,

"Migraine Headaches and Sleep Disturbances in Children," *Headache: The Journal of Head and Face Pain*, April 2003.

Peg Rosen, "The Pain Truth," *Good Housekeeping*, May 2003.

James Sensenig, Jeffrey Marrongelle, Mark Johnson, and Thomas Staverosky, "Treatment of Migraine with Targeted Nutrition Focused on Improved Assimilation and Elimination," *Alternative Medicine Review*, 6, no. 5, 2001.

Internet Sources

ABC Online—Australian Broadcasting Corporation, "Radio National the Health Report, Cluster Headaches." www.abc.net.au., August 9, 1999.

Acupuncture Information, "Testimonials," www.seattleacupuncture. com.

American Headache Society, "Botox Relieves Headaches with Few Side Effects, Suggests Largest Study Yet." www.ahsnet.org.

P. Buckle, P. Kerr, and M. Kryger, "Nocturnal Cluster Headaches Associated with Sleep Apnea, A Case Report," O.U.C.H. Organization for Understanding Cluster Headaches. www.cluster headaches.org.

Cluster Headaches.com, "Cluster Headaches." www.cluster headaches.com.

Larry Deutsch, Cancer Treatment Research Foundation, "Headache, Hypnosis, and Stress: A Case History," ctrf.healthology.com.

Harmonious Healthcare, "Testimonials," www.harmonious healthcare.co.uk.

Lam Kam Sang Medical Research Institute, "Heklin," www. lamkamsang.com.

Migraine Association of Ireland, "Teenagers," www.migraine.ie.

National Headache Foundation, "Over the Counter Pain Medication May Cause Headaches," www.headaches.org.

RemedyFind, "Vitamin B-2 (Riboflavin)," www.remedyfind.com.

Teri Roberts, About Headaches, "Beyond the Pain of Migraine," www.headaches.about.com.

Steven Foster Group, "Ginger," www.herbphoto.com.

World Headache Alliance, "Magnesium Deficiency Linked to Menstrual Migraines in Some Women," www.w-h-a.org.

Index

Picture Credits

About the Author

Barbara Sheen has been a writer and educator for more than thirty years. She writes in English and Spanish. Her fiction and nonfiction have been published in the United States and Europe. She lives with her family in New Mexico. In her spare time, she enjoys swimming, gardening, cooking, and reading.